DANGEROUS
MARINE ANIMALS

DANGEROUS MARINE ANIMALS
THAT BITE, STING, SHOCK, OR ARE NON-EDIBLE

Third Edition

BRUCE W. HALSTEAD, M.D.

Director, International
Biotoxicological Center,
World Life Research Institute
Colton, California

CORNELL MARITIME PRESS
Centreville, Maryland

Library of Congress Cataloging-in-Publication Data
Halstead, Bruce W.
    Dangerous marine animals : that bite, sting, shock,
or are non-edible / Bruce W. Halstead.—3rd ed.
        p.   cm.
    Includes bibliographical references (p.   ) and index.
    ISBN 0-87033-474-3 (pbk.)
    1. Dangerous marine animals.   I. Title.
QL100.H3   1995
591.6′5′09162—dc20   95–14017

Manufactured in Hong Kong
First edition, 1959; Third edition, 1995

To Joy,
and children, Linda,
Sandy, David, Larry,
Claudia, and Shari

CONTENTS

PREFACE

This is the third revision of *Dangerous Marine Animals*, which was first published in 1959. Since that time travel by jet plane has greatly increased accessibility to the most remote sectors of the globe. Accidents related to marine organisms that were once little-known are becoming more commonplace. Oral poisonings and envenomations are occurring with growing frequency. These injuries due to marine animals are a reflection of the greater opportunities for human encounters with these animals in their native environments.

There is also a sobering amount of evidence that extremely toxic marine animals appear to be expanding their range geographically, especially the dinoflagellates. This geographical expansion of outbreaks of poisonings from marine organisms is believed to be an effect of industrial pollution on the environment. There is also evidence that there may be an interaction between chemical pollutants and marine bacteria in the environment which results in the production of some of these poisons. Some oral intoxications are from little-known marine biotoxins. This volume presents for the first time in a handbook of this type a documented outbreak of fatalities caused by eating the Java shark, *Carcharhinus amboinensis*.

The increase in human contacts with marine organisms and the resulting injuries have once again proven the need for an updated, handy reference book that is able to provide a ready source of information regarding the identification, geographical distribution, habits, and noxious characteristics of dangerous marine animals.

Sufficient medical information has been included to be of value to a layman administering first aid as well as a physician. Technical discussions concerning the chemistry and pharmacology of the poisons have been purposely omitted. Every effort has been made to make this a practical guide, keeping technical details to a minimum. If this volume can contribute in a small way to the health and happiness of those working with or just observing marine organisms in their native habitat, it will have fulfilled its mission.

Much of the data presented in this third edition is the result of numerous gifts, grants, and contracts from the following agencies: School of Aerospace Medicine, Air Force Office of Scientific Research and Science Division, Directorate of Science Technology, Department of the Air Force; Office of Naval Research, Bureau of Medicine and Surgery, Department of the Navy; Chemical and Radiological Laboratories, Office of the Surgeon General, Department of the Navy; National Institutes of Health, U.S. Public Health Service; National Science Foundation, Armed Forces Institute of Pathology; U.S. Coast Guard; Pacific Oceanic Fishery Investigations, U.S. Fish and Wildlife Service; Van Camp Laboratories; Food and Agriculture Organization, United Nations; American Philosophical Society; William Waterman Fund of the Research Corporation of America; National Library of Medicine; Pacific Science Board, National Research Council; U.S. National Museum, Smithsonian Institution.

I am deeply indebted to Diana Vivian of our institute staff for her faithful assistance in the preparation of this book. I am also deeply indebted to the following artists and organizations whose works so materially enhance this volume: S. Arita; H. Baerg; L. Barlow; J.H. Barnes; F. Bavendam; A. Bruce Bowker; California Fish and Game; G. Coates; R.S. Criddle; D. Faulkner; Fish Resources of the U.S.S.R.; Al Giddings; R. Given; D.W. Gotshall; Howard Hall; P.A. Hansen; W.D. Hartman; Robert D. Hayes; R. Hildebrand; Paul Humann; L.C. Innes; R.H. Knabenbauer; R. Kreuzinger; T. Kumada; A.R. Loeblich, III, and L.A. Loeblich; D. Ludwig; R.M. Mandojana; Miami Seaquarium; P. Mote; R. Murphy, The Cousteau Society, Inc.; R.F. Myers; Oceanographic Research Institute; D. Perrine; Carl Roessler; T. Rulison; Ron Russo; P. Saunders; Ron and Nancy Sefton; M. Shirao; Tom Stack and Assoc.; R. Straughan; J. Tashijan; Ron and Valerie Taylor; K. Tomito; Vancouver Public Aquarium; G. Webb; and Dave Woodward.

DANGEROUS
MARINE ANIMALS

CHAPTER I

DANGEROUS MARINE ANIMALS— OUR KNOWLEDGE OF THE PAST

The development of the aqualung by the great French diver Jacques Yves Cousteau and his colleagues gave birth to a new area of activity for mankind—skin diving. A new environment was discovered, called by Cousteau the "silent world." Indeed, it is a seemingly silent world, enshrouded in mystery, intrigue, and beauty beyond description. Tropical reefs offer a submarine panorama of colors that seem to vibrate and sparkle. But with this spectacular beauty there is often great peril. In multiplied instances, beauty of form, gracefulness of carriage, lavishness of color seem to go hand in hand with disease and death. Hidden within the delicate lacy fins of the magnificent zebrafish are the needlelike hollow spines that convey deadly venom. Dangers inherent in certain types of marine life are sufficiently great to behoove one to develop an intelligent appreciation of them.

From time immemorial people have depended upon the sea for food, medicine, and clothing and, in recent times, for many industrial and military needs. Philosophers as well as scientists have peered into the depths of the sea and speculated about its contents. What man has been unable to observe directly, his imagination has fashioned in myth and fable. The abysses of the sea and its little-known animal life have served well the interests of writer and storyteller. However, as has been repeatedly shown, much folklore about the sea is based on elements of fact. Therefore, it is of some interest to explore briefly the evolution of our knowledge of dangerous marine organisms.

SHARKS

Sharks and their attacks upon man have stimulated the imagination of writers from antiquity. Probably the earliest reference to man's encounters with sharks is by Pliny the Elder who wrote during the first century of the "cruel combat that sponge fishermen must maintain against the dogfish. . . ." He pointed out that dogfish attack the groins, the heels, and

3

all the white portions of the body. He recommended the best way to frighten off the dogfish was to swim straight for it. Pliny also believed the danger to a diver from shark attacks was greater near the surface of the water than at deeper levels. It is interesting to note that many of Pliny's observations are accepted facts in scientific circles today.

Guillaume Rondelet, famous French physician and naturalist of the Renaissance, frequently lacked facts, but never originality. He describes a footman who was reportedly "observed" running down the beach pursued by a dogfish hot at his heels. Fortunately, the footman struck at the beast with his foot and killed it. In those days dogfish must have been marathon runners! It was Rondelet who also contended that Jonah of the Scriptures was swallowed by a shark rather than a whale.

One of the earliest references to a shark actually attacking a man is in *Septentrionalibus,* written and published about 1555 in Rome by Olaus Magnus. Included in his work is a drawing of several sharks attacking a bather while the bather is being rescued by a "kindly" ray. In 1623, the Dutch navigator Carstenszoon recorded finding sharks, swordfish, and other "un-natural monsters" in the waters near Cape York, Queensland, and alluded to some of their dangers.

According to Dr. Paul Budker, a modern French scholar, sharks were regarded with great fear by sailors working in the Mediterranean during the eighteenth century. Believing that a shark would not attack except in hunger, the sailors felt compelled to throw a loaf of bread to the monster. If this did not suffice, a sailor would have to be lowered by a rope to the surface of the water and look menacingly at the shark—otherwise, it was believed, the shark would grab the vessel with its teeth and devour it.

Probably the greatest number of shark attacks have taken place in Australian waters. The first recorded shark tragedy in that region is by Watkin Tench in *The Narrative of the Expedition to Botany Bay* (1789). Tench refers to a female aboriginal who was bitten in half by a shark in New South Wales several years before. Francois Peron, the naturalist for the Baudin expedition, described a shark attack which occurred at Faure Island, Hamelin Harbour, Western Australia, in 1803.

The question of whether sharks prefer dark or light-skinned victims has been a favorite topic for argument among old "salts." The question appears to have originated with Count Bernard Lacépède, the famous French naturalist, who vigorously debated the subject with some of his colleagues during the early 1800s. Lacépède was of the firm opinion that sharks were attracted to black people, but modern research has shown that sharks seem to be more readily attracted to light-colored objects.

Paul Budker notes in his *La Vie des Requins* that the old slave ships did much to encourage the anthropophagic tastes of sharks. Black slaves were transported in ships in the most primitive, unhygienic, and revolting conditions imaginable. Disease and death were rampant under these circumstances. Trailing in the wake of these vessels of "man's inhumanity to man" were schools of sharks which seemed to await with ghoulish delight their daily ration of human corpses tossed over the side. After one severe storm on a run between Mozambique and Bourbon, France, more than fifty slaves suffocated because of the necessity of closing the hatches. With callous disregard for human life, a mariner wrote these words in the log of the vessel: "What a windfall for the sharks!"

Although man's involvement with sharks and shark attacks dates back to ancient times, most authoritative data on the subject have appeared in technical publications only within the past few decades. The work of Dr. Gilbert P. Whitley (1940), *The fishes of Australia. The sharks, rays, devil-fish, and other primitive fishes of Australia and New Zealand,* contains a great deal of valuable and interesting information regarding the habits, identification, and folklore connected with sharks. His work also includes a list of all the reported shark attacks in Australia to the time of publication in 1940.

The increased loss of surface vessels and aircraft, and the resulting high incidence of shark attacks during World War II, pointed up the need for an effective shark repellent. Through the combined efforts of the U.S. Office of Scientific Research and Development; U.S. Navy and Army Air Corps; the National Research Council; and various civilian organizations, such as the American Museum of Natural History; Woods Hole Oceanographic Institution; Scripps Institute of Oceanography; Marine Studios, Inc.; New York Zoological Society; University of Florida; and the Calco Chemical Corporation, an intensive search was made for a satisfactory deterrent. Experiments were conducted feeding sharks bait with the various chemicals to be tested. Controls were also run feeding the sharks bait without the repellent, and the results of the two tests were then compared. After testing more than seventy different compounds, it was found that no more than four were deserving of further attention: decomposing shark meat, maleic acid, copper sulfate, and copper acetate. It was subsequently shown that the potent factor in the decomposing meat was ammonium acetate. It was later decided that a dye should be added in order to hide the swimmer from view. Finally, a chemical packet was developed which combined a nigrosine dye with copper acetate. This compound was later given the popular but somewhat misleading name, *shark chaser*. According to the research reports conducted at that time, this compound was reputed to be highly effective under normal feeding conditions of the shark. More recent studies have shown that the repellent is generally ineffective under circumstances when it is needed most. Nevertheless, it was the best repellent available for many years and was used extensively on life preservers for the U.S. Armed Forces. The material was commercially produced by the Shark Chaser Chemical Company, San Pedro, California.

About the time that American researchers were conducting their investigations on shark repellents, similar studies were going on in Australia under the auspices of the Commonwealth Scientific and Industrial Research Organization. Because of the high incidence of shark attacks along the coast of New South Wales, Australia, the local government instituted a Shark Menace Advisory Committee to investigate methods of protecting bathers from shark attacks. As a result of their studies, a program in meshing was begun, consisting of laying a long rope net overnight near the beach and removing it by trawler in the morning. This technique has proved to be highly efficacious and is still employed in Australia, South Africa, and in other areas where sharks are considered a menace to bathers.

One of the earliest and best documented serious publications to deal with the overall problem of shark attacks appeared in 1958 by Victor M. Coppleson, the noted Australian physician who died in 1963. His well-illustrated book, entitled *Shark Attack*, contains numerous accounts of attacks, resultant medical injuries, methods of dealing with an attacking shark as well as identification, habits, and distribution of dangerous shark species. Coppleson's work is a classic in its field and should be read by anyone interested in the subject.

Probably the greatest impetus to the scientific investigation of shark attacks and related medical problems was the result of the American Institute of Biological Sciences' Conference on Shark Repellents held in New Orleans (April 1958), sponsored jointly by the AIBS, Tulane University, and the Office of Naval Research and Bureau of Aeronautics of the U.S. Navy. Although the main topic of the conference was concerned with the efficacy of the "shark chaser," which had been developed by the U.S. Naval Research Laboratory during World War II, it soon became evident to everyone that there was a vast gap in basic knowledge of the biology, habits, and even identification of dangerous sharks. Out of this conference came a series of recommendations concerning the need for further information on shark behavior, ecology, taxonomy, physiology, morphology, and particularly the teleceptor sensor mechanisms of sharks.

An international committee known as the Shark Research Panel was appointed to formulate tentative recommendations for a broad scientific program dealing with the shark hazard problem under the capable chairmanship of Perry A. Gilbert, and originally consisted of Lester R. Aronson; Bruce W. Halstead; Carl L. Hubbs; Arthur W. Martin; Leonard P. Schultz; J. L. B. Smith; Stewart Springer; Tohru Uchida; F. G. Wood, Jr.; and Gilbert P. Whitley. A group of thirty-four scientists internationally recognized for their knowledge of sharks participated in the original conference. One of the significant outgrowths of this conference was the ultimate establishment of the worldwide Shark Attack File. Initially, the Shark Attack File was housed at the Smithsonian Institution under the direct supervision of Leonard P. Schultz. Later it was moved to the Mote Marine Laboratory in Sarasota, Florida. Gilbert served as chairman of the Shark Research Panel during the almost twelve years of its existence. The Shark Attack File contained data on a series of 1,165 case histories covering the years 1941 through 1968, and was ultimately expanded to include 1,652 cases. Final analysis of the Shark Attack File was done by a group of statisticians and programmers of the U.S. Navy's Bureau of Medicine and Surgery, and the final publication appeared as a Special Technical Report (Contract No. N00014-73-C-0252), dated October 31, 1973, under the authorship of H. David Baldridge, entitled *Shark Attack Against Man.* A popularized, paperback version of Baldridge's work, *Shark Attack,* was published in 1974. A distillate of some of the more pertinent findings obtained from the Shark Attack File appear in the section of this handbook dealing with sharks.

With the expansion of underwater recreational activity and the maintenance of large oceanariums, knowledge of other traumagenic marine organisms has increased significantly. Some of this additional knowledge is reflected in this latest revision.

STINGING MARINE ANIMALS

Knowledge of stinging marine animals dates back to the days of classical antiquity. Aristotle, writing from 348 to 322 B.C., made reference to the stinging ability of stingrays. Nicander, Greek poet and physician of the second century B.C., reported that the sting of the stingray caused "gangrene of the wounded flesh." Pliny the Elder, carried away with the subject, reported that the deadly stingray, called Trygon, was able to kill a tree by driving its sting into one of the roots! He also mentions the serious wounds produced by the weeverfish.

Numerous scientific and popular reports are to be found in early literature relative to the dangers of stings from venomous fishes, but serious scientific research on the subject was not conducted until the time of Dr. A. Bottard, a French scientist, who wrote the first monograph on the venom organs of venomous fishes, *Les Poissons Venimeux,* which was published in 1889. Several scientists previously worked on the venom organs of weever-fish, but Bottard was the first to approach the subject in a more or less organized manner. Another important contribution to the field of marine venomology was that of the great French physician Albert Calmette, whose classic *Venoms, Venomous Animals, and Antivenomous Serum-Therapeutics* was published in 1908.

One of the earliest known occupational illnesses of divers caused by the biological hazard of stinging marine animals is the so-called sponge fisher-man's disease. This disease, frequently manifested by a severe burning skin rash with areas of painful ulcerations, for many years was believed to be due to the handling of sponges. Finally, Dr. S. G. Zervos demonstrated in a series of scientific articles published in France in 1903, 1934, and 1938 that the disease was not due directly to sponges, but rather to coming into contact with the stinging tentacles of small sea anemones adhering to the sponges.

We are largely indebted to Dr. H. Muir Evans, an English surgeon, for our early knowledge of the venom apparatus of the stingray. Much of Dr. Evans's medical practice was concerned with the care of fishermen in Lowestoft, England, who came to him with wounds they had received from weevers, spiny dogfish, and stingrays. The stimulus Dr. Evans received from his patients goaded him to study the venomous nature of these fish on a scientific basis. Thus a new horizon opened in medicine, described by Evans in an interesting manner in his *Stingfish and Seafarer* (1943). Those who have engaged in research on venomous fishes in America owe much to the challenge provided by the writings of this fine old English surgeon of Lowestoft. Serious students interested in stinging marine organisms will also receive much benefit from the outstanding volume of Marie Phisalix, *Animaux Venimeux et Venins* (1922), and the brilliant writings of E. N. Pawlowsky, *Gifttiere and Giftigkeit* (1927).

Modern marine venomologists are indebted to the numerous contribu-tions of Australian scientists who have studied the identification, morphology, and toxicology of some of the oceans' most dangerous stinging creatures inhabiting the southwestern Indo-Pacific region. Much of this research is discussed in the well-illustrated volume by John B. Cleland and R. V. Southcott, *Injuries to Man from Marine Invertebrates in the Australian Region.* Carl Edmonds has produced a valuable handbook on the *Dangerous Marine Animals of the Indo-Pacific Region.* Noteworthy also is the valuable Japanese work *Marine Toxins,* written by one of the world's foremost marine biotoxicologists, Yoshiro Hashimoto. This book, the last contribution of a great scientist, was completed just prior to his death.

A comprehensive review and monographs on poisonous and venomous marine animals of the world have been written by the author (Halstead, 1965, 1970, 1978, 1988, 1991), and by Halstead, Auerbach, and Campbell (1990). See section on suggested reading, page 257.

MARINE ANIMALS POISONOUS TO EAT

The danger of eating poisonous marine organisms was known in the time of the Pharaohs of ancient Egypt, during the Toltec civilization in ancient Mexico, and in Biblical days when Moses led the children of Israel out of the land of Egypt with the warning ". . . and whatsoever hath not fins and scales ye may not eat; it is unclean unto you" (Deut. 14:9-10). This advice is still recommended in modern American military survival manuals.

Emperors of ancient Japan forbade soldiers to indulge in the most poisonous of all fishes, the deadly puffer, called in Japan, the fugu. Those caught eating this scaleless delicate morsel lost their entire inheritance. Similar prohibitions were issued by Alexander the Great to his soldiers.

Peter Martyr, the great historian of the West Indies, specifically refers to the danger of the ciguatera type of fish poisoning. This form of poisoning supposedly developed in fishes as a result of their eating the poison machineel berry—a theory which continues to persist today, but is without scientific foundation. As a result of eating poisonous fishes sold to him by friendly savages in New Caledonia, Captain Cook almost terminated his famous world voyage in 1776.

Through the centuries, hundreds of articles written by explorers, missionaries, physicians, naturalists, and scientists describe the dangers of eating molluscs, fishes, and other marine organisms at certain seasons of the year under given circumstances. The French, Russian, Japanese, and American navies have called attention to the medical importance of these organisms. It is estimated that during World War II more than four hundred

Japanese military personnel lost their lives in Micronesia from the eating of fresh tropical reef fishes. A most unusual piece of toxicological research on the poisonous fishes of Micronesia was conducted by the Japanese scientist, Dr. Yoshio Hiyama in 1941. Visiting the Marshall and Saipan Islands under the most trying of circumstances, he found that large numbers of the reef fishes of these islands were deadly for humans to eat. It was Dr. Hiyama's work that served as a basis for much of the subsequent research on poisonous fishes conducted in the United States and elsewhere.

The origin of oral fish intoxicants, fish that are poisonous to eat, has always been a mystery, and continues to elude scientists. For centuries it has been known that a fish species may be edible in one geographical area and deadly poisonous in another. There are a number of different types of oral fish poisons. Some of them are extremely rare, whereas others are of common occurrence in tropical insular areas of the world. Scombroid fish poisoning, ciguatera, and puffer poisoning continue to remain significant public health problems on many tropical islands, and threaten the development and utilization of shore fisheries in areas wherever these public health problems are endemic.

During the last few decades a great deal of scientific effort has been directed toward obtaining an understanding of the chemical and pharmacological properties of ciguatoxin, saxitoxin, scombroid poisoning, and tetrodotoxin (the cause of puffer poisoning). The chemical structure of saxitoxin and tetrodotoxin is now well-known, and probably more than five hundred scientific articles concerning their pharmacological and neurophysiological properties have been written. The biogenesis of ciguatoxin is gradually unfolding, and it has been demonstrated that dinoflagellates are involved. The cause of scombroid fish poisoning is now known.

The present handbook deals with only a cursory review of facts regarding animals of marine origin that are poisonous to eat. However, an attempt has been made to present those facts of crucial significance to the aquatic enthusiast. One of the first things to remember is that not everything in the sea is edible, and that one should be cautious about eating inshore fishes in tropical island areas without first checking with the local inhabitants. Otherwise, that fish dinner about to be eaten might be the last one! If mankind is to continue to utilize the resources of the sea, greater efforts must be expended to attempt to unravel the mysteries hidden in its depths.

WHAT OF THE FUTURE?

As we glance at the dimly lit pages of the past, we are reminded of the debt of gratitude the scientific community owes to scientists of yesterday. Old musty archives continue to contribute valuable medical data to those who go into the depths of the sea. Our applied knowledge regarding most marine creatures is still very meager. Moreover, our knowledge will continue to remain so until basic medical and marine biological research is permitted to join hands in pushing back the frontiers of ignorance.

The reader should keep in mind that as we enter the sea and match wits with its death-dealing creatures, there is an ever-increasing amount of scientific evidence that these same noxious organisms and their poisons may serve as sources of the life-giving antibiotics, anticancer, and other indispensable therapeutic agents of tomorrow. These organisms must be considered as more than mere marine biological hazards—they are the vast chemical reserves of the future.

But now for the cold realities of today—dangerous marine organisms—their noxious effects, treatment, or, better yet, how to avoid them!

CHAPTER 2

MARINE ANIMALS THAT BITE

SHARKS

Sharks are the marine animals generally feared by most swimmers and divers. With the plethora of publications and movies dealing with shark attacks, real and fictitious, public awareness of the potential danger of sharks has reached an unprecedented high. During the past few decades a great deal of valuable information on the biology of sharks has come to light; however, the scientific community continues to suffer from a general lack of knowledge concerning these magnificent, toothy creatures. The following is a summary of some of the more pertinent information concerning sharks and their predatory habits. Much of this data is based on the International Shark Attack File investigations.

GENERAL

There are about 250 species of sharks known to ichthyologists, but only 27 species appear to have been definitely incriminated in attacks on man. Dangerous sharks are almost cosmopolitan in their geographical distribution (fig. 2-1). However, most shark attacks have occurred between latitudes 47° south and 46° north. The most northerly unprovoked shark attack occurred in the upper Adriatic Sea, and the most southerly attack took place off South Island, New Zealand. About 54 percent of the documented attacks have taken place in the Southern Hemisphere. Shark attacks are most common in warm temperate and tropical waters, occurring in areas where the water temperature is above 68°F (20°C).

Shark attacks tend to be seasonal depending upon weather conditions, warm water temperatures, and time of day when swimmers are most plentiful. Studies show that there is greater danger during late afternoon and at night, when sharks are most actively feeding.

Sharks range in size from some of the smaller species, which mature at a length of only 15.2 centimeters (6 inches), to the giant whale shark, which

Fig. 2-1. Map showing shark attack zones. (After Coppleson).

may attain a length of more than 15.2 meters (50 feet). Fortunately for the human species, the giant whale shark feeds primarily on planktonic organisms and its dentition is not suitable for larger objects.

The natural food of the larger, dangerous sharks consists mainly of large fishes, other sharks, seals, and a variety of marine organisms. If compelled to generalize about the dietary habits of these animals, one may assume that if the shark is more than 1.2 meters (4 feet) in length, has adequate teeth, and if there is food or blood in the water, it is potentially dangerous to any human being nearby.

The sex of a shark can be determined by the presence or absence of claspers, appearing as modified pelvic fins in the male to form intromittent organs. The claspers are used by the male to convey the semen to the female. All sharks practice internal fertilization. There are three different ways by which sharks are born: from eggs (oviparous), alive (viviparous), or from eggs hatched within the uterus and then born alive (ovoviviparous). The method of birth employed varies with the species of the shark. The general external anatomy of a shark is shown in figure 2-2.

DENTITION

Sharks are characterized by having several rows or series of teeth in each jaw. The number of series of teeth in actual use at any one time varies from one to five in different species of sharks. Examination of the inside of the

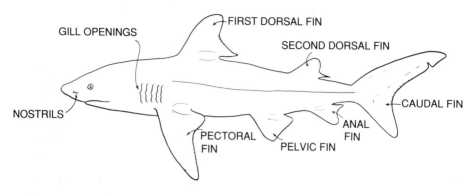

Fig. 2-2. External anatomy of a typical shark.

jaws will reveal that there are one to several additional reserve series lying in a reversed position. The reserve teeth point up in the upper jaw and down in the lower jaw. As functional teeth are lost, those of the next series move forward to replace them (fig. 2-3). This process of tooth replacement continues throughout the life of the shark. Teeth may be replaced singly in some shark species, or as an entire series in others. A series of teeth that forms a continuous cutting edge is generally replaced as an entire series. The replacement process usually requires several days to a week or more.

The force of a shark bite is enormous. Actual measurements made with the use of a shark bite meter have shown that some of the larger sharks, such as the great white (*Carcharodon carcharias*), can exert a force of about 18 metric tons per square inch of tooth surface (18.2 metric tons per square 2.5 centimeters).

SENSORY SYSTEM

The intelligence of a shark is generally considered to be of a low order, but this is of little consolation to anyone threatened by an attack. The means employed by sharks to detect their prey, food, or injured animals is a subject of prime importance to anyone concerned with shark attacks. Sharks have the usual sensory organs consisting of eyes, an auditory apparatus, and nose. The visual acuity of sharks appears to be better than previously believed, both for color and for distinguishing an object that is moving past a dark background. Vision is believed to be the prime sensory organ employed at a distance of 15.2 meters (50 feet) or less, depending upon the clarity of the water. At distances greater than 15.2 meters, olfaction and other sensory organs appear to be of greater importance in food detection. The musculature of the eye permits the shark to maintain a constant visual field even when it is

Fig. 2-3. Jaws of the **Great White Shark**, *Carcharodon carcharias*. Anterior view. Length of shark about 2.4 meters (8 feet). Courtesy Oceanographic Research Institute, Durban, South Africa.

twisting, turning, or moving ahead. Since sharks spend much of their time at depths where lighting conditions are poor, some shark species have a special mirrorlike reflecting layer (*tapetum lucidum*) that is situated under the retina and reflects incoming light back through the retina. This mechanism permits optimum utilization of light in a dimly lit aquatic environment. Thus, the eyes of a shark are highly effective for its predatory activities.

Sharks have an amazingly acute sense of smell. As every comparative anatomist knows, the olfactory lobes of sharks are highly developed and comprise a major segment of their brain. Olfaction enables a shark to detect blood and food in the water—probably at levels as minute as parts per billion or even more.

Sharks also have gustatory chemoreceptors or taste buds providing them with a sense of taste and permitting them to discriminate between food and other objects. These gustatory receptors undoubtedly play an important role in determining the dietary activities of sharks.

Another important set of sensory organs in sharks are the chemoreceptors in the skin, sometimes referred to as the "common chemical sense." These skin chemoreceptors provide the shark with the ability to perceive substances of an irritating nature, changes in salinity, water movements, and other chemical changes in the water. Knowledge concerning the precise function of these chemoreceptors could be of importance for the future development of chemical shark repellents.

One of the most important teleceptor devices in the shark is its "hearing" mechanism. Sharks detect sounds by means of the labyrinth (inner ear), the lateral line, and a group of specialized sensory receptors known as the *ampullae of Lorenzini*. With the use of these highly sensitive teleceptors, sharks have a phenomenal ability to detect low frequency vibrations in the water. This is why sharks can readily detect at great distances such disturbances as those caused by fish struggling and people swimming. The movements of sharks are controlled to a large extent by means of their combined teleceptor systems. The swimmer should keep in mind that sharks are always "listening" and are sensitive to any vibrational disturbance in the water.

When all of the various sensory systems of sharks are taken into consideration, it becomes obvious that the shark is a highly integrated "computerized" sensory marvel, possibly without equal either in the aquatic environment or on land.

FEEDING PATTERNS

The feeding habits or patterns of sharks are quite variable but for the sake of convenience can be grouped into two general types: The first, the *normal feeding pattern* (fig. 2-4) can best be described as a situation in which one or several sharks are seen moving about with seemingly purposeful movements either in quest of food or actually feeding. In many instances the movements of the shark appear to be slow and determined, but at times may be erratic and swift moving. The swimming pattern, approach, and the final attack may vary with the species and circumstances. The *frenzied feeding pattern* (fig. 2-5) most frequently develops after a catastrophic event such as an explosion, sinking of a vessel, the crash of a plane in the water, or the sudden availability of large quantities of food. When any of these conditions is present, the entire feeding characteristics of sharks may rapidly change. The frenzied feeding pattern is further enhanced if sharks begin to congregate in large numbers. Under these conditions the swimming behavior of sharks becomes exceedingly erratic. They have been observed swimming vertically up to the surface,

Fig. 2-4. *Top*, **Bull Shark**, *Carcharhinus leucas*. Young specimen. About 1.5 meters (5 feet) in length. *Bottom*, **Dusky Shark**, *Carcharhinus obscurus*. About 1.5 meters (5 feet) in length. Sharks are in a "normal" swimming pattern. Courtesy Oceanographic Research Institute, Durban, South Africa.

Fig. 2-5. **Dusky Sharks,** *Carcharhinus obscurus.* Young specimens. About 1.5 meters (5 feet) in length, in a frenzied feeding pattern. Chunks of fish are in the water. Sharks in this frenzied behavior become very dangerous and erratic. Courtesy Oceanographic Research Institute, Durban, South Africa.

snapping at floating objects, and then suddenly plunging to the bottom of a lagoon, literally banging their noses on the bottom, and snapping savagely at anything in sight. It is during periods such as this that most repellent devices become useless and may even aggravate the situation. Cannibalism was observed in one instance during frenzied conditions, stimulated by an underwater blast, in which a school of snappers (*Lutjanidae*) had been killed. While one large shark fed on a snapper that had been caught under a coral head, a second shark moved into the scene and in one quick gulp ripped out the belly of the first shark. Within a few moments the hapless shark was completely devoured by other members of the pack who joined the killing. The species involved was the gray reef shark (*Carcharhinus amblyrhynchos*) at Jaluit, Marshall Islands.

ATTACK PATTERN

In most instances (about 63 percent) the attacking shark was not seen by the victim prior to contact. In some instances sharks have been observed swimming very erratically just prior to making a rush on the victim. At the same time the pectoral fins were extended downward and the back of the shark was bowed into a hunched position. Then the shark was seen to swim stiffly with its whole body, its head moving back and forth almost as much as its tail. This behavior preceded a swift pass at the victim, a type of activity designated as "agonistic or combative behavior."

There is no single behavior performance that typifies the attack pattern of all sharks. Almost every conceivable type of activity has been observed under the heading of aggressive behavior. Shark attacks on man are sometimes preceded by one or more contacts, which range from gentle bumping to violent collisions. At times these violent impacts can be severe enough to knock the victim completely out of the water.

Sharks have sometimes been known to single out an individual in a crowd of swimmers and continue to attack that individual to the exclusion of all other persons, including those who attempt to rescue the victim. However, because of the unpredictability of sharks, it is difficult to anticipate any specific type of attack approach.

Provoked versus Unprovoked Attacks: A significant number of shark attacks have occurred because of *provoked* encounters, such as spearing, poking at the shark, grabbing the shark by the tail, tantalizing the shark with fish, blocking off an escape passageway, or by some other means that obviously annoyed the shark. Encounters of this type are very foolhardy and should be avoided. Nevertheless, *unprovoked* attacks have taken place in which the victim appeared to be minding his own business and there appeared to be little or no reason for the attack—other than a hungry shark and the presence of a dainty morsel.

Color or Pattern Attraction: There are no firm, general conclusions that can be given about color and patterns relative to their attraction for sharks. However, it has been observed that bright highly reflective dyes, pigments, bright metallic objects, and contrasting color patterns may attract sharks. On the other hand, one should attempt to avoid appearing as a marine mammal or some other organism on which sharks normally feed. This situation has been found to occur when surfers are resting or paddling on a surfboard. Obviously, what attracts a shark under one circumstance is possibly a deterrent in another set of environmental conditions. It should be kept in mind that the visual acuity of a shark may not always be the best under adverse environmental conditions. Consequently, when operating under conditions of poor visibility, such as murky water or restricted lighting, color and pattern may be matters of increased importance in attracting sharks and precipitating an attack.

INCIDENCE OF SHARK ATTACKS

Evaluation of the Shark Attack File revealed a documented incidence of about twenty-eight attacks per year, but there is reason to believe the overall incidence is much higher. The reason for this apparent discrepancy is that many attacks occur in remote areas of the world and pass by unreported. However, it is doubtful the actual incidence attains the 100 attacks per year that is sometimes given.

The overall case fatality rate based on documented records of a series of 1,165 attacks was 35 percent. Previous estimates were placed at a much higher figure.

SPECIES OF SHARKS DANGEROUS TO HUMAN BEINGS

The following is a partial listing of sharks known to be dangerous that have been incriminated in attacks on human beings. There are additional species known to be dangerous, but they have not been included because attacks by them are relatively uncommon. The families are arranged in alphabetical order.

FAMILY CARCHARHINIDAE

This family consists of Gray Sharks, Whaler Sharks, and Requiem Sharks. This is the largest family of living sharks, comprising at least thirteen genera, and numerous species. Many species of this family are considered to be dangerous and several of them have caused human fatalities.

SILVER TIP SHARK, *Carcharhinus albimarginatus* (Rüppell) (fig. 2-6). This is an aggressive shark that attains a length of 3.4 meters (12 feet). It is widely distributed throughout the warm waters of the western Indian, western Pacific, western northern Atlantic, and eastern Pacific oceans. The silver tip shark is commonly found in inshore to offshore areas with a preference for offshore tropical islands, coral reefs, and banks. The silver tip shark has twelve to fourteen rows of teeth, with which this animal can fatally injure its prey. Its distinctive features include a moderately long and broadly rounded snout, with the first dorsal fin moderately large and semifalcate with a pointed or narrowly rounded apex and a posterior margin curving ventrally from fin apex. The color of this shark is dark gray above, sometimes

Fig. 2-6. *From top*, **Silver Tip Shark**, *Carcharhinus albimarginatus* (Rüppell). **Gray Reef Shark,** ▶
Carcharhinus amblyrynchos (Bleeker). **Blacktip Reef Shark**, *Carcharhinus melanopterus* (Quoy
and Gaimard). Paintings by R. H. Knabenbauer.

with a bronze tinge, white below, all fins with conspicuous white tips and posterior margins, and an inconspicuous white band on flanks. This shark is considered to be dangerous, but records of attacks on humans are unavailable.

GRAY REEF SHARK, *Carcharhinus amblyrhynchos* (Bleeker) (see fig. 2-6). This species has been frequently designated as *Carcharhinus menisorrah*, which is now believed to be an entirely different species. It has been repeatedly incriminated in human attacks. Frequently found in large groups, the gray reef shark may become very aggressive if food is in the water. It can readily enter into a frenzied feeding pattern, at which time it may become quite dangerous. Attaining a length of 2.1 meters (7 feet or more), the gray reef shark is abundant in lagoons of coral islands in the Indo-Pacific and Indian Oceans. It is grayish above, paler to whitish below, and its fins are grayish to blackish, but not black tipped.

BRONZE WHALER, *Carcharhinus brachyurus* (Günther) (figs. 2-7, 2-13). This shark, incriminated in human attacks, attains a length of about 2.7 meters (9 feet). An active open-ocean species, it ranges off the coast of New South Wales and southern Queensland, Australia. It is colored bronze to golden above and creamy white below.

GALAPAGOS SHARK, *Carcharhinus galapagensis* (Snodgrass and Heller) (see fig. 2-8). Incriminated in human attacks, the Galapagos attains a length of 2.4 meters (8 feet). Found in the West Indies and in the eastern Pacific westward to the Indian Ocean, it is probably the most abundant shallow water shark in the eastern Pacific. Colored gray above and cream below, it is often mottled with gray, with the tips of the pectoral and first dorsal darker.

BULL SHARK, *Carcharhinus leucas* (Valenciennes) (fig. 2-7). This species is believed to be synonymous with *Carcharhinus nicaraguensis* (Lake Nicaragua shark), *Carcharhinus zambezensis* (Zambezi shark), and *Carcharhinus gangeticus* (Ganges River shark), and several other closely related members—all of which are dangerous to man and have been repeatedly incriminated in human attacks. The bull shark attains a length of about 3.6 meters (12 feet) and inhabits the warmer waters of the Atlantic, Pacific, and Indian Oceans. These sharks also penetrate freshwater and are found in Lake Nicaragua; Lake Izabel, Guatemala; and Lake Jamoer, New Guinea; and extend into the upper reaches of the Amazon and the rivers of Australia, Iraq, and Southeast Africa, as far as 1126 kilometers (700 miles) inland from

Fig. 2-7. *From top,* **Bronze Whaler,** *Carcharhinus brachyurus* (Günther). **Bull Shark,** *Carcharhinus leucas* (Valenciennes). **Great Blue Shark,** *Prionace glauca* (Linnaeus). **Whitetip Oceanic Shark,** *Carcharhinus longimanus* (Poey). Paintings by R. H. Knabenbauer.

the sea. It is usually a slow swimming shark except when stimulated by food. Gray above and white below, its fins are dark tipped in the young.

WHITETIP OCEANIC SHARK, *Carcharhinus longimanus* (Poey) (figs. 2-7 and 2-14). This is an active, almost fearless shark also charged in human attacks. It attains a length of about 3.6 meters (12 feet). It is widely distributed throughout the warm waters of the Atlantic, Pacific, and Indian Oceans. As a deep water species it seldom, if ever, comes close to shore. Distinctive characteristics are the broadly rounded apex of the first dorsal fin, the convexity of the posterior outline of the lower caudal lobe, and a very short snout in front of the nostrils. Colored bluish, gray, or brown above and yellowish to whitish below, its fins are white tipped mottled with gray. Juveniles may have dusky-tipped fins.

BLACK WHALER, *Carcharhinus macrurus* (Ramsey and Ogilby) (figs. 2-8 and 2-15) The black whaler, incriminated in human attacks, attains a length of 3.6 meters (12 feet). It is found both offshore and in shallow water areas, inhabiting the waters along the east coast of Australia. It is colored sandy and dark gray above, whitish below, and the tips of its fins are often dusky.

BLACKTIP REEF SHARK, *Carcharhinus melanopterus* (Quoy and Gaimard) (see fig. 2-6). This shark attains a length of about 1.8 meters (6 feet) and is common about coral reefs. Widespread throughout the tropical Indo-Pacific, extending into the Red Sea, the blacktip reef shark is brownish to blackish above, paler to white below, and its fin tips usually appear strikingly black. The shark, although charged in human attacks, can generally be frightened away by making overt movements toward it.

DUSKY SHARK, *Carcharhinus obscurus* (Lesueur) (fig. 2-8). This shark attains a length of about 3.6 meters (12 feet). Although primarily a pelagic shark, it may enter shallow coastal areas. The species has been recorded from the warm Atlantic, to the eastern Pacific, and western Indian Oceans. It is blue gray to pale gray above and white below, the undersides and tips of the pectoral fins are grayish to dusky. The dusky shark is a seasonal migratory species.

TIGER SHARK, *Galeocerdo cuvier* (Lesueur) (fig. 2-9). This species is second highest in the number of shark attacks on human beings; at least twenty-seven documented attacks are credited to it. The tiger shark is known to attain a length of at least 5.4 meters (18 feet), and probably more, but most large specimens range from 3.6 to 4.5 meters (12 to 15 feet). The

◀ Fig. 2-8. *From top*, **Lemon Shark**, *Negaprion brevirostris* (Poey). **Galapagos Shark**, *Carcharhinus galapagensis* (Snodgrass and Heller). **Black Whaler**, *Carcharhinus macrurus* (Ramsey and Ogilby). **Dusky Shark**, *Carcharhinus obscurus* (Lesueur). Paintings by R. H. Knabenbauer.

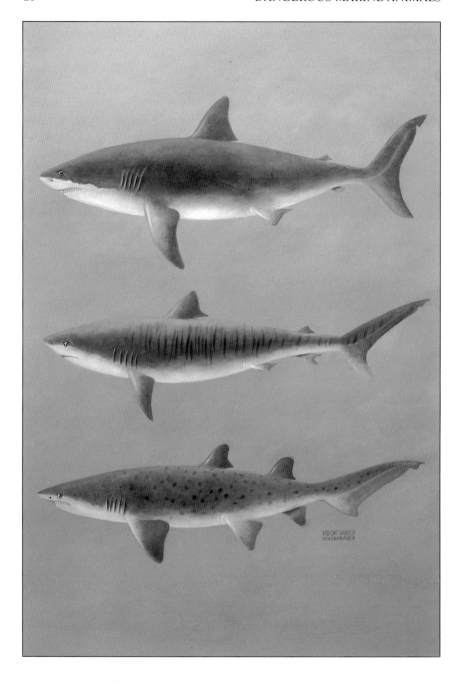

distinctive characteristics of the tiger shark are its teeth, short snout, and sharply pointed tail. Its color is gray or grayish brown, darker above than on sides and belly. The oblique or transverse blotches on the back and fins are present mostly in younger specimens, tending to fade with maturity. Large specimens are patterned only on the caudal peduncle or not at all.

The tiger shark may be sluggish, but under the proper stimulation can be a vigorous and powerful swimmer. The tiger shark is widespread throughout tropical and subtropical regions of all oceans, inshore and offshore alike, and may enter river mouths. It is said to be one of the most common of the large sharks in the tropics.

LEMON SHARK, *Negaprion brevirostris* (Poey) (figs. 2-8 and 2-16). Documented human attacks have been reported for the lemon shark. It attains a length of about 3.3 meters (11 feet). Differing from other members of this family, its distinctive features are a second dorsal fin almost as large as the first, a broadly rounded snout, and unique teeth. The lemon shark is primarily an inshore species, commonly found in saltwater creeks, bays and sounds, and around docks. This shark ranges from New Jersey to northern Brazil, and to tropical West Africa, but is especially common in the waters about Florida and the Keys. It has been studied extensively because of its ability to survive in captivity.

GREAT BLUE SHARK, *Prionace glauca* (Linnaeus) (figs. 2-7 and 2-17). This shark attains a length of 3.6 meters (12 feet) or more. *Prionace* is largely a pelagic species, living in the open sea, but may also be found along coastal areas. This shark appears as a slow swimmer when not in pursuit of food, but becomes an active and aggressive fish when stimulated by food. The color of the shark is indigo blue above, slightly lighter on the sides, and white below. It is widely distributed throughout tropical and warm temperate oceans.

WHITETIP REEF SHARK, *Trianodon obesus* (Rüppell)(fig. 2-10). Although rarely incriminated in human attacks, it is considered to be potentially dangerous. It attains a length of about 2.4 meters (8 feet). The whitetip reef shark is frequently found around reefs, coral atolls, and along shorelines. Widespread throughout the warm waters of the Pacific and Indian Oceans and the Red Sea, this shark is distinguished by the conspicuous white markings on the first dorsal pectoral and upper caudal fins. Its colors are gray above and white below. It is sometimes confused with the whitetip oceanic shark, which differs in form and coloration, and is a deep water species.

◄ Fig. 2-9. *From top*, **Great White Shark**, *Carcharadon carcharius* (Linnaeus). **Tiger Shark**, *Galeocerdo cuvier* (Peron and Lesueur). **Sand Shark**, *Carcharius taurus* Rafinesque. Paintings by R. H. Knabenbauer.

Fig. 2-10. **Whitetip Reef Shark**, *Trianodon obesus* (Rüppell). A very common small reef shark, it is usually quite timid, but capable of attacking. Valerie Taylor is seen here photographing the shark in the Coral Sea. Attains a length of 2.4 meters (8 feet). Photograph courtesy of Ron and Valerie Taylor.

FAMILY CARCHARIIDAE

This family includes a small group of typical sharks, having five gill openings, an anal fin, two dorsal fins of almost equal size, and no fin spines. Only one genus is known, with about six species, at least two of which have been incriminated in human attacks.

GRAY NURSE SHARK, *Carcharias arenarius* Ogilby (fig. 2-11). Said to be swift and savage in making its attacks, the gray nurse shark, charged in human attacks, attains a length of 4.5 meters (15 feet). As an inshore species, it lives close to the bottom of waters about Australia. Its color is similar to the *Carcharias taurus*, brownish above and dirty white below.

SAND SHARK, *Carcharias taurus* Rafinesque (fig. 2-9). A comparatively sluggish shark with a voracious appetite, it feeds very actively at night. It lives mostly near the bottom as an inshore species. The sand shark attains a

Fig. 2-11. *From top*, **Gray Nurse Shark**, *Carcharias arenarius* Ogilby. **Mako Shark**, *Isurus* ▶ *oxyrinchus* Rafinesque. **Mackerel Shark**, *Lamna nasus* (Bonnaterre). **Nurse Shark**, *Ginglymostoma cirratum* (Bonnaterre). Paintings by R. H. Knabenbauer.

Fig. 2-12. *Top*, **Wobbegong Shark**, *Orectolobus ornatus* (DeVis). *Bottom*, **Smooth Hammerhead**, *Sphyrna zygaena* (Linnaeus). Length 4 meters (13.1 feet). Paintings by R. H. Knabenbauer.

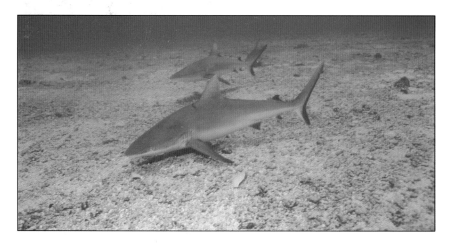

Fig. 2-13. **Bronze Whaler**, *Carcharhinus brachyurus* (Günther). Length 2.7 meters (9 feet). Photograph courtesy of Carl Roessler. Taken at Coral Sea, Australia.

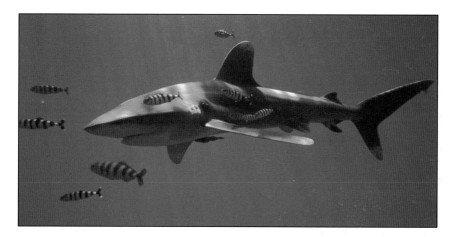

Fig. 2-14. **Whitetip Oceanic**, *Carcharhinus longimanus* (Poey). Length 3.6 meters (12 feet). Photograph courtesy of Al Giddings.

Fig. 2-15. **Black Whaler**, *Carcharhinus macrurus* (Ramsey and Ogilby). Photograph courtesy of Ron and Valerie Taylor.

length of about 3.1 meters (10 feet). It inhabits the Mediterranean, Atlantic, and the Indian Ocean along eastern Africa. It is gray or brown above, paler to dirty white below, and sparsely flecked on back and sides. Its fins are colored with brownish spots.

Fig. 2-16. **Lemon Shark**, *Negaprion brevirostris* (Poey). Length 3.3 meters (11 feet). Photograph courtesy of D. Perrine.

Fig. 2-17. **Great Blue Shark**, *Prionace glauca* (Linnaeus). Photograph courtesy of Howard Hall.

FAMILY ISURIDAE

This family comprises only three genera, *Carcharodon, Lamna,* and *Isurus,* and a total of about a half dozen species or less. All the members of this family are large sharks and potentially dangerous.

GREAT WHITE SHARK, *Carcharodon carcharias* (Linnaeus) (fig. 2-9). This shark is reputed to be the most dangerous of all sharks, despite the claim by some shark experts that the white shark is a "man-biter" and not a "man-eater." It is believed by some that attacks on man are due to a case of mistaken identity. Nevertheless, this shark is credited with more attacks on humans than any other shark species. It attains a length of 6.1 meters (20 feet) or more. The white shark is characterized by an obtusely conical head, heavy-bodied, strongly lunate caudal fin, and large triangular serrate teeth. Colored grayish brown, gray or bluish above, and dirty white below, it usually has a black spot on its body at the rear of the pectoral fin base. The outer tips of the pectoral fins are blackish. The great white shark ranges into the tropical and temperate oceans of the world; it is generally oceanic, but may come into shallow water. It is inclined to be solitary.

MAKO SHARK, *Isurus oxyrinchus* Rafinesque (figs. 2-11 and 2-18). A dangerous species incriminated in human attacks, this oceanic inhabitant may come close to shore. It is one of the most active of all sharks, leaping when hooked. It tends to be an aggressive and savage biter with a fearsome-looking set of jaws. It has been involved in more attacks on boats than any other shark species. Attaining a length of 3.6 meters (12 feet), it inhabits all tropical and temperate oceans. Its colors are dark blue-gray or blue above and white below.

MACKEREL SHARK, *Lamna nasus* (Bonnaterre) (fig. 2-11). Generally regarded as a potentially dangerous species, it tends to be a sluggish swimmer, but may become active and aggressive when in pursuit of food. This shark attains a length of 3.1 meters (10 feet) or more. Inhabiting temperate regions of all oceans, it is bluish gray or gray above and white below.

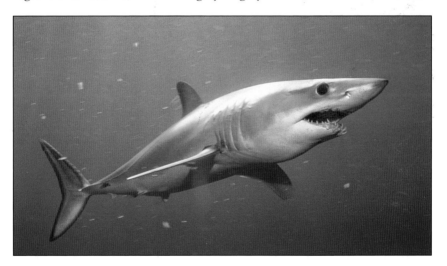

Fig. 2-18. **Mako Shark**, *Isurus oxyrinchus* (Rafinesque). Length 3.6 meters (12 feet). Photograph courtesy of Howard Hall.

FAMILY ORECTOLOBIDAE

This is a large family, including carpet sharks, nurse sharks, and wobbe-gongs, with about twelve genera and numerous species, inhabiting the Indo-Pacific and Red Sea. They are small-sized, inhabiting reefs and shallow water. Several species have been incriminated in attacks on humans.

NURSE SHARK, *Ginglymostoma cirratum* (Bonnaterre) (figs. 2-11 and 2-19). This species attains a length of 4.2 meters (14 feet). It is sluggish, often found lying on the bottom in schools. Human beings come in contact with it only when inadvertently swimming near the shark or stepping on it. Nurse sharks inhabit the warm waters of the Atlantic and the Pacific Oceans. Closely related species are found in the Indian Ocean.

WOBBEGONG, *Orectolobus ornatus* (DeVis) (figs. 2-12 and 2-20). This and related species have been incriminated in human attacks. Attaining a length of 2.1 meters (7 feet), the wobbegong has a prominent color pattern of blotches, spots, and marblings, together with fleshy lobes which tend to camouflage it in its shallow-water habitat of weed-covered rocks. Its general color is gray or brown, and it inhabits eastern and southeastern Australia.

FAMILY SPHYRNIDAE

This family is characterized by their peculiar flat, wide, hammer- or bonnet-shaped heads, which clearly distinguish them from all other sharks. How-

Fig. 2-19. **Nurse Shark**, *Ginglymostoma cirratum* (Bonnaterre). Length 4.2 meters (14 feet). Photograph courtesy of Al Giddings.

Fig. 2-20. **Wobbegong Shark**, *Orectolobus ornatus* (DeVis). Photograph courtesy of Ron and Valerie Taylor.

ever, with the exception of the morphology of the head, they appear to be more closely related to carcharhinids. There are thought to be two genera, but some ichthyologists place them in a single genus, *Sphyrna*, which is composed of about seven species. They are found in warm waters of all oceans. A number of attacks have been made on humans by hammerheads, but the precise species involved is unknown.

SMOOTH HAMMERHEAD SHARK, *Sphyrna zygaena* (Linnaeus) (figs. 2-12, 2-21). The hammerhead shark tends to be a leisurely swimmer, frequently observed swimming slowly at the surface as though basking in the sun. It attains a length of about 4.2 meters (14 feet). A common species found in tropical and warm temperate waters of all oceans, its color is dark olive or brownish gray above, paler to white below, with tips of the fins dusky or black.

Prevention: There are numerous techniques that have been recommended over the years in an attempt to prevent shark attacks. None of the

Fig. 2-21. School of Hammerhead Sharks, Sea of Cortez, Baja California. Photograph courtesy R. Murphy, The Cousteau Society, Inc..

methods recommended are 100 percent effective, but it is generally conceded that there are some basic principles which, if followed, can be helpful in minimizing a nasty encounter. One must always realize that sharks are unpredictable and that every possible precautionary measure should be used when swimming in warm temperate or tropical oceans; sharks are likely to be present and listening, even though they may not be visible to the swimmer.

Whenever possible, swim with a group or a buddy. If isolated, you may become a prime target for an attack.

If dangerous sharks are known to be in an area, it is advisable to stay out of the water, particularly if the water is turbid. If a dangerous shark is encountered, try to exit with slow, purposeful movements rather than by a series of panicky splashes, keeping in mind that sharks are keenly sensitive to distress signals set up by low frequency vibrations in the water. If you want to attract a shark, keep splashing with erratic, irregular movements. It is advisable to face the shark at all times and not to turn your back on the beast.

Do not provoke an attack by spearing, poking, grabbing, riding, or hanging onto the tail of a shark. The skin of a shark is rough, covered with denticles similar to very coarse sandpaper, and capable of inflicting severe skin abrasions. Even a relatively small shark can inflict serious injuries when provoked. Treat large and small sharks with respect. Blood attracts and excites sharks. Therefore, do not enter or remain in the water with a bleeding wound. Women should avoid swimming in shark-infested waters during their menstrual periods.

Avoid murky or turbid water in which there is poor visibility. The swimmer has a slight edge on the situation with good visibility. Refrain from swimming far from shore in deep water, in deep water channels, or in drop-offs likely to be inhabited by large sharks.

Check the water carefully before jumping or diving off a boat. Avoid swimming at dusk and at night when sharks are most likely to be feeding. Do not swim in the vicinity of garbage dumps.

When spear fishing, do not tie the fish to your body. Toss the dead fish into a boat or raft, or anchor the fish some distance from where you are diving.

Wear dark protective clothing. Bright, shiny objects and highly contrasting clothing tend to attract sharks and barracuda.

Sharks will frequently circle their intended victim several times before coming in for the strike. Therefore, get out of the water or into a boat as rapidly as possible. Try to use a rhythmic beat with the feet, moving steadily toward the boat or shore, and try not to panic. If wearing scuba gear, remain submerged until reaching the boat. You are more vulnerable at the surface. When possible, move to a defensive terrain with a coral reef or some other immovable object to your back, and face the aggressor.

In the event of an air or sea disaster, do not abandon your clothing when entering the water. Clothing will not only afford some protection from abrasions, but will help to preserve body heat. Try to remain as quiet as possible in order to conserve energy. Attempt to use a lifeboat or a raft when possible. Do not trail arms or legs over the side of the raft. Do not fish from a raft when sharks are nearby.

Repellents: Despite the questionable value of the U.S. Navy Shark Repellent (Shark Chaser), which is comprised of a black dye and lead acetate, it should be used if available. Experimental studies have shown that some shark species will tend to avoid the dye, whereas others are unaffected by it.

If your group is threatened by a shark, form a tight circle and face the shark. If an encounter is inevitable, hit the shark on the snout or in the eye with whatever object is available. Use your hands or feet only as a last resort. A shark billy, a stick tipped with a sharp metal object such as a nail, has been found to be useful in pushing off sharks.

The value of a bang stick, smoky, or powerhead, is a matter of controversy. This is an explosive device for delivering a shot or slug to the brain or some other vital organ of the shark. Firing is accomplished by forcefully driving the triggering mechanism into the head or body of the shark. When properly applied, the shot is capable of instantly killing a large shark. The problem in using a bang stick is that it should not be used by a novice. It is not only a dangerous weapon, but is only effective when dealing with a solitary shark. When working in a school of sharks, it may stimulate the sharks to go into a frenzied feeding pattern. The blood and noise in the water will attract more sharks and thus compound an already precarious situation.

A CO_2 gas dart gun exists which is used primarily to disturb the buoyancy characteristics of a shark. With the use of the gas dart gun, a CO_2 charge is fired into the abdomen of the shark causing the animal to be unable to control his movements and to float helplessly to the surface. However, this device is of questionable value in defense against a charging shark. Moreover, it is difficult to penetrate the tough hide of the shark and may aggravate the animal still further. Properly applied, it may serve as a useful defensive tool, but should be used with caution.

Electrical devices of various types have been proposed, but currently, none of them appear to be of practical value. Various poisons and drug agents are also in the experimental stage and are as yet of little value.

The use of *meshing* has been the most practical and effective method to date of controlling beach areas inhabited by dangerous sharks and visited by swimmers. This involves the use of large gill nets which are submerged parallel to the beach and close to the surf line. Sharks become enmeshed in the nets and die.

Dr. Scott Johnson of the U.S. Naval Undersea Center has developed a shark screen, which is a water-filled plastic sack suspended from the surface by means of flotation rings. The sack is large enough for an adult to roll into and float loosely. The sack thus eliminates most of the teleceptor sensory stimulation of the shark and thereby provides a limited amount of protection by means of camouflage. Unfortunately, a device such as this has limited application, but under proper circumstances would be of value.

Sonic repellent vibrations have been experimented with, but apparently are unsuccessful so far. One area that needs further examination is the possibility of developing chemical repugnatorial agents. Unfortunately, this field of research has suffered from a lack of adequate support. It is questionable that a completely effective anti-shark measure will ever be developed for the swimmer and diver.

Medical Aspects: Bites from sharks are severe and death is usually due to massive hemorrhage and shock (figs. 2-22 and 2-23). The case fatality rate is about 35 percent.

Fig. 2-22. Body of seventeen-year-old boy killed by a **Great White Shark**, *Carcharodon carcharias* (Linnaeus). The attack occurred on December 7, 1952, at 1400 hours, about 22.8 meters (25 yards) from shore, just beyond the breaker line, off the tip of Point Aulone, Monterey, California. The water temperature was 12.7°C and the water visibility was about 2.4 meters (8 feet). The boy was struck by the shark from the front with such force as to throw him out of the water to the level of his thighs. The victim was then forcefully dragged down into the water by the shark. The victim then surfaced, screaming in the midst of a bloody patch of water. The shark surfaced so as to be clearly seen by an observer on the shore and was estimated to be upwards of 4 meters (13 feet) in length. The victim was rescued by a fellow swimmer, but died en route to the shore. Examination of the body revealed that the bites inflicted were all below the hips. The major wound involved excision of the lower part of the right buttock and most of the muscle mass on the dorum of the thigh, almost to the knee. No bones were broken, but the lower part of the ischium was laid bare, and the femur was exposed for about three quarters of its length. The femoral artery was completely severed. The left leg was also severely lacerated. The boy died of massive blood and tissue loss. The drawing was prepared from the photos obtained at the time of the autopsy. This gruesome illustration graphically depicts the nature of the bite of the great white shark. This drawing and account are based on the original report by R.L. Bolin, *Pacific Science,* 8:105-108, 1954. Painting by R.H. Knabenbauer.

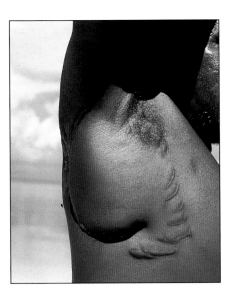

Fig. 2-23. Showing scars of a shark bite on a victim who survived the attack. Identification of shark unknown. The shark was believed to have been about 2.4 meters (8 feet) in length. Ninigo Islands, Bismarck Archipelago. Courtesy of A.M. Cousteau.

Treatment: The initial first aid given to the patient is of the utmost importance. Failure to apply properly these measures may result in the needless death of the victim. A person who has been bitten should be removed from the water as rapidly as possible. In some instances the control of bleeding may have to be instituted in the water if there is any unavoidable delay in removing the victim from the water. However, it should be kept in mind that blood in the water is an intense stimulation to sharks and encourages further attacks.

The patient should be treated immediately on the beach by controlling bleeding by means of a tourniquet or with the use of a pressure bandage. In applying a tourniquet the patient should be lying down and the limb elevated. A piece of material should be tied around the limb using clothing or padding to avoid pinching the skin. A stick is then passed through the knot and twisted to tighten the tourniquet until the bleeding stops. Do not tighten the tourniquet beyond that point. Tie the stick in such a fashion that the tourniquet does not release. Loosen the tourniquet every twenty minutes. *Keep in mind that if the tourniquet is left too long the limb may become gangrenous and necessitate amputation.*

It is important during these procedures to reassure the patient continually. Position the patient on the sand with his head lowermost. Cover the patient lightly with a towel or thin blanket. Send for an ambulance. Do not give anything by mouth at this time. The patient should remain unmoved for about thirty minutes regardless of treatment. Overzealous rushing to the hospital can be dangerous and reduce the patient's chances of survival.

If there has been excessive bleeding, the initial intravenous therapy should be administered on the beach or boat. Intravenous solutions to be considered are Group O-Rh negative blood, plasma, 5 percent albumen, normal saline, 5 percent dextrose and water, or other plasma expanders. Attempts to control homeostasis and to combat shock are of primary concern at this time. Sedation using morphine (15 mg) or its equivalent intravenously may be required. After control of shock, the patient should be carefully transported to the hospital for further emergency treatment.

The treatment required will vary with the individual case, but there are a few general considerations of importance. Cardiopulmonary resuscitation is of primary concern—if required. Once the patient's condition has stabilized, the resulting trauma should be carefully assessed and definitive treatment instituted. Radiological examination may be required to determine the amount of bone damage. Debridement of the wound is usually needed. Bacteriological cultures should be made and sensitivity tests conducted. Some species of marine bacteria may be quite virulent and resistant to most antibiotics. The wound should be photographed and documented. Conservative surgical techniques should be employed and an attempt made to preserve as much tissue as possible. In many cases early skin grafting may be required. If available, hyperbaric oxygen therapy should be employed during the early healing period.

GIANT DEVIL RAY OR MANTA
FAMILY MOBULIDAE

The GIANT RAY, Manta birostris (Donndorff), may attain a spread of more than 6 meters (20 feet), and a weight of more than 1,588 kg (3500 pounds) (fig. 2-24). It does not possess a caudal sting. When harpooned, it is able to tow a small launch for several hours. The manta is not aggressive and is dangerous only because of its huge size. Several deaths have been reported of helmet divers whose airline became fouled in the cephalic fins and "wings" of mantas that apparently came over to investigate the bubbles. Like most sharks, their skin is covered by coarse dermal denticles which can inflict a severe abrasion of the skin if one were to brush up against them. They are generally seen swimming or basking near the surface of the water with the

Fig. 2-24. **Giant Devil** or **Manta Ray**, *Manta birostris* (Donndorff). Photograph courtesy of Dave Woodward.

tips of their long pectoral fins curling above the surface. Occasionally, they are seen leaping out and falling back into the water with a tremendous splash. Mantas are primarily plankton feeders, but may eat crustaceans and small fishes at times. Their color is reddish or olivaceous-brown to black above, and light beneath. Mantas are found in tropical-subtropical belts in both hemispheres. Although some investigators believe that there may be as many as ten different species of mantas, they have been more recently grouped together under the single species *Manta birostris*.

BARRACUDA
FAMILY SPHYRAENIDAE

Reports concerning the danger of attacks from barracuda are conflicting, probably due to the fact that there are about twenty species, which differ greatly in their aggressiveness. True barracuda are members of the family Sphyraenidae and are voracious carnivores. Some of these species are harmless because of their small size. This is true of a large school of *Sphyraena chinesis* (Lacépède), in the Marshall Islands, where divers consistently swam among them without concern, and where in no instance did they attempt to attack; nor on the other hand did the barracuda demonstrate undue fear of the divers. The same can be said for the PACIFIC BARRACUDA, *Sphyraena argentaea* Girard.

However, under the proper circumstances, the GREAT BARRACUDA, *Sphyraena barracuda* (Walbaum) (fig. 2-25), is said to be an exceedingly pugnacious and dangerous foe. According to E.W. Gudger (1918), who made an extensive study of the biology and habits of the great barracuda, this fish is feared more than sharks in some areas of the West Indies. Donald P. De Sylva has published an extensive review of barracuda attacks on man in his book, *Systematics and Life History of the Great Barracuda* Sphyraena barracuda *(Walbaum)*, (Miami: University of Miami, Rosenstiel School of Marine & Atmospheric Science, 1972). In this book, in which twenty-nine attacks are listed, fatalities occur, but were usually due to blood loss.

The great barracuda may attain a length of 1.8-2.4 meters (6-8 feet) and a weight of 48.1 kilograms (106 pounds). His mouth is large and filled with enormous knifelike canine teeth (fig. 2-26). A swift swimmer, striking rapidly and fiercely, *Sphyraena barracuda* is found in the West Indies and Brazil, north to Florida, and in the Indo-Pacific from the Red Sea to the Hawaiian Islands. In general, species of barracuda are widely distributed throughout tropical and subtropical waters of the world.

Skin divers report that barracuda are attracted to anything which enters the water, particularly bright-colored objects. Barracuda depend almost entirely on sight, and usually make a single attack, which in most instances is non-fatal. They will follow divers by the hour, but have seldom been known to attack an underwater diver.

Medical Aspects: Barracuda wounds can be differentiated from those of a shark, since the former are straight cuts consisting of two nearly parallel

Fig. 2-25. **Great Barracuda**, *Sphyraena barracuda* (Walbaum). Drawing by T. Kumada.

Fig. 2-26. Jaws of the **Great Barracuda**, *Sphyraena barracuda* (Walbaum). Side view, from a fish about 1.8 meters (6 feet) in length. Taken at Al Ghardaqa, Red Sea. W.L.R.I. photo.

rows of tooth marks, whereas sharks produce a parabolic wound curved like the shape of their jaws (see fig. 2-3).

Treatment: Bites should be treated in the same manner as shark bites.

Prevention: Barracuda are attracted by bright-colored objects and will strike at any speared fish that a diver may be carrying. When swimming in waters inhabited by the great barracuda, precautions should be taken not to attract their interest unduly. When swimming in the company of the great barracuda, treat it with respect and caution—this may be that rare one that bites.

MORAY EELS
FAMILY MURAENIDAE

This family contains some twenty or more species. They are largely confined to tropical and subtropical seas. The TROPICAL MORAY EEL, *Gymnothorax javanicus* (Bleeker) is found in the Indo-Pacific (fig. 2-27). Several temperate

Fig. 2-27. **Tropical Moray Eel**, *Gymnothorax javanicus* (Bleeker). Moray eels possess numerous sharp, fanglike teeth which are capable of inflicting a nasty bite. They are most likely encountered by divers reaching into holes in the reef. The flesh of some tropical species may be deadly poisonous. This species is found in the Indo-Pacific region. Length 1.5 meters (5 feet). Courtesy of Douglas Faulkner.

Fig. 2-28. Skull and jaws of a typical moray eel, *Gymnothorax*, showing the sharp canine teeth. Drawing by T. Kumada.

zone species are known, for example *Gymnothorax mordax* (Ayres), the moray eel of California, and *Muraena helena* Linnaeus of Europe. Although moray eels are notoriously powerful and vicious biters, they seldom attack unless provoked. When wounded, they can inflict severe lacerations with their narrow muscular jaws, which are armed with strong, knifelike, or crushing teeth (fig. 2-28). They may retain their bulldoglike grip until death. Their powerful muscular bodies are covered by a tough leathery skin which is not readily penetrated by a knife. Morays are unbelievably slippery and difficult to grasp. Some of the larger species may attain a length of 3.1 meters

Fig. 2-29. Bite from a moray eel. Bites of this type are usually the result of an un-suspecting diver sticking his hand in the mouth of a moray eel. Look before you poke! This diver got off easy. Guam, Mari-ana Islands. Photograph courtesy of R.C. Schoening.

(10 feet), and more than 30.5 centimeters (1 foot) in diameter. Morays are bottom-dwellers, commonly found lurking in holes, and writhing snakelike through crevices, under rocks or corals (fig. 2-29).

Medical Aspects: Wounds produced by moray eels are usually of the tearing, jagged type.

Treatment: The principles involved in the treatment of shark bites are also applicable here.

Prevention: Wounds from moray eels are most likely to be encountered when poking around crevices, in holes, or under coral or rocks inhabited by them. Poke your hand into a hole with caution!

NEEDLEFISH
FAMILY BELONIDAE

Although needlefish, sometimes referred to as a saltwater garfish, superficially resemble the freshwater garfish, they are phylogenetically unrelated. Needlefish are inhabitants of tropical seas, and are found in bays, inshore areas, and at times in deeper water, but are largely surface swimmers. Needlefish have a long slender body and possess two pointed elongated jaws that are filled with sharp unequal teeth (figs. 2-30 and 2-31). Some of the larger needlefish may attain a length of 1.8 meters (6 feet). Generally, when

Fig. 2-30. **Needlefish**, *Tylosaurus crocodilus* (Lesueur). There are several closely related species, and all have been involved in attacks on humans. In most instances, the victim was impaled by the javelin-like jaws. Several persons have died from chest wounds in which the jaws penetrated the victim's heart. Large specimens may attain a length of 1.8 meters (6 feet). Photograph courtesy of R.F. Myers.

Fig. 2-31. Closeup of the head and jaws of *Tylosaurus crocodilus* (Lesueur). Courtesy of R.F. Myers.

needlefish are undisturbed, they move along with an undulating motion of the body, but when excited, can scull rapidly over the surface of the water. Needlefish are frequently attracted by light at night and may leap out of the water in the direction of the light. They have also been observed leap-frogging over objects in the water. It is during these periods of excitation that they may inflict their wounds by plunging their sharp beaks into anyone in their flight path.

Medical Aspects: Needlefish have inflicted serious injuries and even fatalities to humans. These injuries have consisted of severe puncture wounds to the chest, involving heart and lungs, abdomen, arms, legs, and neck. In 1977, a ten-year-old Hawaiian boy was killed while net fishing at Hanamulu Bay, Kauai, when a needlefish, believed to be *Strongylura gigantea* (Temminck and Schlegel), jumped over the net and penetrated his brain.

Treatment: Wounds are of the puncture variety and usually require prompt surgical care. The possibility of bacterial contamination must be considered. The patient should be taken to the nearest hospital or physician for treatment.

Fig. 2-32. **Giant Grouper**, *Promicrops lance-olatus* (Bloch). Photograph courtesy of A. Powers. Taken near Sydney, Australia.

Prevention: Needlefish injuries are most likely to be encountered when night light fishing. Avoid being in a flight pattern between needlefish and the light. A person should be constantly aware of the potential danger from these fish when working at the surface in tropical waters.

GIANT GROUPER OR SEABASS
FAMILY SERRANIDAE

GIANT GROUPER or SEABASS, *Promicrops lanceolatus* (Bloch), a Queensland grouper, is reputed to be the largest fish inhabiting Australian waters. It is said to attain a length of more than 3.6 meters (12 feet) and a weight of more than 335 kilograms (750 pounds). Grouper tend to be unusually curious, bold, and voracious feeders. They are considered as a potential hazard primarily because of their large size, cavernous jaws, and fearless attitude. Certainly, they do not constitute a hazard in the sense that sharks do. Grouper are most frequently found lurking around rocks, caverns, old wrecks, etc. Large grouper may be toxic to eat (fig. 2-32).

Medical Aspects: Wounds produced by grouper would be similar to shark bites, but probably with less tissue loss.

Treatment: Similar to handling shark bites.

Prevention: Examine large caves or caverns before entering.

SALTWATER OR ESTUARINE CROCODILE
FAMILY CROCODYLIDAE

The SALTWATER or ESTUARINE CROCODILE, *Crocodylus porosus* (Schnei-der) (fig. 2-33) is one of the most dangerous of marine organisms. It ranges over an extensive geographical area including India, Sri Lanka, southern China, Western Islands, Malay Archipelago, Palau, Solomon Islands, and northern Australia. Although it usually inhabits coastal mangrove swamps, river mouths, and brackish inlets, the vast range of this crocodile is the result of its extensive excursions out to sea. Adult crocodiles have been observed swimming at sea, completely out of sight of any land (fig. 2-34).

The saltwater crocodile may attain a length of more than 6.1 meters (20 feet). The back of this species is colored a brassy yellow, spotted, and blotched with black. However, older specimens may appear to be uniformly black on the back. The ventral surface is whitish or pale yellow. The stable diet of the beast is terrapins, frogs, fishes, prawns, crabs, and even water beetles. At night crocodiles enter rice paddy fields and marshy lands in search of prey, and during these excursions, they frequently capture large mam-mals, in some instances human beings.

The ferociousness of this crocodile is well-documented. In areas where it is endemic, it has taken numerous human lives. The crocodile frequently

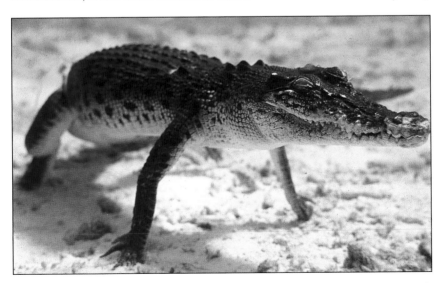

Fig. 2-33. **Saltwater Crocodile**, *Crocodylus porosus* (Schneider). Photograph courtesy of D. Ludwig.

Fig. 2-34. **Saltwater Crocodile**, *Crocodylus porosus* (Schneider). Few creatures are better equipped for grasping and tearing flesh than the crocodiles. This species has been responsible for many human deaths. They are capable of moving with surprising speed on land. The saltwater crocodile is usually found in mangrove swamps in shallow waters. Attains a length of 6.1 meters (20 feet) or more. Taken at Palau, Micronesia. Photograph courtesy of D. Ludwig.

attacks with a loud hissing sound, grasps the victim with a powerful bite, and, in the process of dismembering the victim, drowns it with a quick twirling movement of the body. It may also sweep an animal off its feet by a blow of the tail.

Medical Aspects: Human deaths are reported each year in areas where this reptile is abundant (fig. 2-35). Once the victim is seized, only rarely is escape possible. Crocodile bites are usually serious, extensive in nature, and result in massive tissue loss. Oftentimes crocodile bites are more extensive than many shark bites. Death is usually due to the severity of the wounds inflicted and drowning.

Treatment: Treatment is seldom possible, but if the opportunity presents itself, treat the patient in the same manner as shark bites. It should be kept in mind that crocodile wounds are frequently contaminated by bacterial pathogens, and if not treated properly may result in gas gangrene or tetanus.

Prevention: Avoid swimming in murky, brackish water inlets, swamps, and river mouths inhabited by saltwater crocodiles. Crocodiles are extremely

Fig. 2-35. Crocodile bite from *Crocodylus porosus* (Schneider). Bite on upper torso. Taken at Wyndham, W. Australia. Photograph courtesy of G. Webb.

fast on their feet and are excellent swimmers. They can inflict a lethal blow with their tails. Avoid all possible contact with these savage brutes in either daylight or dark.

SEA LIONS AND SEALS, ORDER PINNIPEDIA

Under ordinary circumstances, sea lions (fig. 2-36) are usually not aggressive. However, during the breeding season, the large bulls become irritable and may attack a diver, particularly if provoked. Bites from sea lions have been reported.

Seals are generally docile, but the bulls become quite irritable during the breeding season and may inflict a serious wound. Seals need to be treated with respect (fig. 2-37).

KILLER WHALES
FAMILY DELPHINIDAE

The KILLER WHALE, *Orcinus orca* (Linnaeus) (fig. 2-38), has long been designated as a "ruthless and ferocious killer," but more recent studies apparently fail to justify this reputation. Also, people's attitudes have changed

Fig. 2-36. **California Sea Lion,** *Zalophus californianus* Lesson. Sea of Cortez. Photograph courtesy of Howard Hall.

Fig. 2-37. Sea lions do bite, as shown in this photo. The diver provoked a male sea lion, which inflicted a bite. Fortunately, sea lions make a quick lunge and then retreat. Photograph courtesy of R.C. Schoening.

in favor of the killer whale because they have had opportunities to observe this magnificent mammal living in oceanariums. Found in all oceans ranging from tropical to polar latitudes, the killer whale is the largest and one of the more intelligent of the living dolphins. They usually travel in pods of up to

Fig. 2-38. **Killer Whale**, *Orcinus orca* (Linnaeus). Painting by R. H. Knabenbauer.

forty individuals, are predators, fast swimmers, and feed on a wide variety
of marine organisms, including invertebrates, fish, birds, seals, walrus, and
even some of the larger whales. Killer whales attain a length of 9.1 meters
(30 feet). They have a powerful set of jaws equipped with a formidable array
of cone-shaped teeth (fig. 2-39) that are directed toward the throat and are
thereby adapted for grasping and holding food. The crushing power of these
jaws is immense. The killer whale is quite capable of snapping a seal or
porpoise in half with a single bite. Despite their playful antics in the secluded
atmosphere of an oceanarium, they must continue to be regarded with
considerable respect as a potentially dangerous marine animal in the wild.
Most experts are convinced that killer whales do not go in search of humans
for food; however, there is always the possibility the whale might mistake a
human being for some other food.

Fig. 2-39. Looking into the mouth of the killer whale. This whale attains a length of 9.1 meters (30 feet). Note the powerful set of cone-shaped teeth. The crushing power of these teeth is enormous. Photograph courtesy of Vancouver Public Aquarium.

GIANT TRIDACNA CLAMS
FAMILY TRIDACNIDAE

The so-called giant, or killer clams, *Tridacna gigas* (Linnaeus)(fig. 2-40) abound in tropical waters. Some of them attain huge proportions, measuring 1.4 meters (4.6 feet) long and weighing 203 kilos (507 pounds). Although accidents from giant, or killer clams, are rare, one should learn to recognize them and to avoid catching a foot or hand between the two valves of the clam. Drownings have occurred from divers accidentally stepping into the open valves and becoming trapped. Several accidents of this type are said to have taken place along the Great Barrier Reef of Australia. In order to release the victim, a knife must be inserted between the valves of the clam and the adductor muscles severed (fig. 2-41).

Fig. 2-40. **Giant Tridacna Clam**, *Tridacna gigas* (Linnaeus). Attains a length of 1.4 meters (4.6 feet) and a weight of 203 kilos (507 pounds). Great Barrier Reef, Australia. Photograph courtesy of H. Hall.

Fig. 2-41. Painting of giant *Tridacna* clam showing where to cut the adductor muscles. Painting by R.H. Knabenbauer.

OCTOPUS

FAMILY OCTOPODIDAE

The OCTOPUS, *Octopus apollyon* Berry, named after the Greek God Apollo. This octopus inhabits the Pacific Northwest region. May attain a length of more than 8.8 meters (29 feet). Despite its large size, it tends to be docile; on occasions, however, it may bite. This is a very intelligent animal and at times outsmarts its would-be captors. Its color pattern and form vary greatly depending upon the background and circumstances in which the animal is found. See figure 3-36 on page 85.

CHAPTER 3

MARINE ANIMALS THAT STING: INVERTEBRATES

Venomous marine invertebrates, or marine animals without backbones that inflict their injuries by stinging, can be grouped into six major categories, or phyla:

1. Porifera—Sponges
2. Coelenterata—Hydroids, Jellyfishes, Corals, and Sea Anemones
3. Mollusca—Univalve shellfish and Octopuses
4. Annelida—Stinging or Bristle Worms
5. Echinodermata—Sea Urchins
6. Ectoprocta—Bryozoa or Moss Animals

SPONGES, PORIFERA

Sponges are primitive multicellular animals of simple and loose organization. They are found from shallow intertidal beaches to the deepest oceanic abyss. The soft cells of the body are supported by an internal skeleton consisting of tiny needlelike spicules of silica, calcium carbonate, or a fibrous substance known as spongin. The siliceous and carbonate spicules may serve as an irritant when brought in contact with the skin. In some sponge species there may be a toxic substance involved. The identification of sponges is based upon the shape and composition of these spicules. Many sponges are difficult to identify. It is estimated that there are about four thousand species, some of which are found in freshwater. Some sponges are capable of inflicting an extremely painful dermatitis involving erythema, edema, vesicle formation, a skin infection, peeling of the skin, and a delayed anaphylactoid reaction. Skin infections may become serious medical problems. The two sponge species discussed here are notorious stingers.

FAMILY DESMACIDONIDAE

RED MOSS SPONGE, *Micronciona prolifera* (Ellis and Solander)(fig. 3-1). The size is variable. This sponge is found along the Atlantic coast of the United States from Cape Cod to South Carolina.

FAMILY TEDANIIDAE

FIRE SPONGE, *Tedania ignis* (Duchassaing and Michelotti)(fig. 3-2). The size is variable. It inhabits the West Indies.

Medical Aspects: It is usually difficult to separate a reaction due to spicule irritant dermatitis from an early hypersensitivity reaction. The skin should be gently dried and a layer of adhesive tape applied to attempt to peel away any superficial spicules. An alternative method is to apply a commercial facial gel, which may be used as a "peel." Five percent acetic acid (vinegar) soaks should be applied for fifteen to thirty minutes, three to four times daily. If acetic acid is not available, isopropyl alcohol (40 to 70 percent) may be substituted. The remainder of treatment is generally much the same as for severe poison ivy dermatitis. Although corticosteroid lotions may help to relieve the secondary inflammation, they appear to be of little value in the

Fig. 3-1. **Red Moss Sponge**, *Microciona prolifera* (Ellis and Solander). This sponge is found along the Atlantic coast of the United States from Cape Cod to South Carolina. Size is variable. Painting by R.H. Knabenbauer.

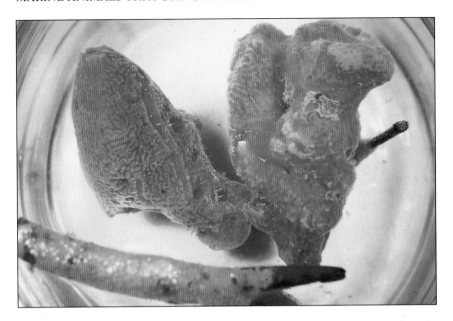

Fig. 3-2. **Fire Sponge**, *Tedania ignis* (Duchassaing and Michelotti). Inhabits the West Indies. The size is variable. Courtesy of W.D. Hartman.

initial decontamination. Following the initial decontamination, a mild emollient cream or steroid preparation may be applied to the skin. If the allergic component is severe, particularly if there is weeping, crusting, and blister formation, systemic corticosteroids should be used. Severe itching may be controlled with an antihistamine.

Prevention: Avoid touching sponges with your bare hands. Divers working in tropical waters should be completely clothed with protective lightweight diving suits of some type, nylon or a lightweight neoprene suit, in order to avoid contact with stinging sponges. Most sponges are harmless, but some of them are capable of producing the painful dermatitis described above.

COELENTERATES, COELENTERATA

The coelenterates (Coelenterata), which include the hydroids, jellyfishes, corals, and sea anemones, are simple, many-celled organisms. In addition to a number of other technical characteristics, they all possess tentacles equipped with nematocysts or stinging cells. It is the stinging cells of the coelenterates which are of concern to the skin diver.

The coelenterates are divided into three principal classes:

Fig. 3-3. **Fire Coral,** *Millepora alcicornis* (Linnaeus). Section of Fire Coral and painful rash inflicted by it. The rash subsided after about six hours. Size is variable. Taken at the Marine Biological Station, University of Cairo, at Al Ghardaqa, Red Sea. Courtesy of D. Ollis.

HYDROIDS, HYDROZOA

Hydroid (Hydrozoa) are commonly found growing in plumelike tufts on rocks, seaweeds, and pilings. It is estimated that there are about 2,700 species. Some of the more common stinging members of this group are the following:

STINGING OR FIRE CORAL—FAMILY MILLEPORIDAE

STINGING or FIRE CORAL, *Millepora alcicornis* (Linnaeus) (fig. 3-3). This false coral is generally found living among true corals along reefs in the warm waters of the tropical Pacific Indian Ocean, Red Sea, and Caribbean Sea. The height of the colony is variable.

FIRE CORAL, *Millepora dichotoma* (Forskål). This species resembles *Millepora alcicornis.*

FAMILY PLUMULARIIDAE

STINGING SEAWEED, *Aglaophenia cupressina* (Lamouroux) (fig. 3-4). This hydroid is found in many parts of the tropical Indo-Pacific region. The height of the colony may reach 12.7 centimeters (5 inches). It has an almost

Fig. 3-4. **Stinging Seaweed**, *Aglaophenia cupressina* (Lamouroux). This hydroid is erroneously termed a "seaweed," but despite its general appearance, it is an animal. Colony 12.7 centimeters (5 inches) in height. Courtesy of Ron and Valerie Taylor.

Fig. 3-5. A. **Stinging hydroid**, *Lytocarpus nuttingi* Hargitt. Height of colony is up to 10 centimeters (4 inches). Courtesy of D. Gotshall.

seaweedlike appearance, hence its common name. It is light brown in color and capable of causing nettlelike stings with red welts and vesicles which may last several days.

STINGING HYDROID, *Lytocarpus nuttingi* Hargitt (fig. 3-5). There are several closely allied species of *Lytocarpus,* all of which are capable of inflicting painful stings. Do not let their beautiful plumelike appearance

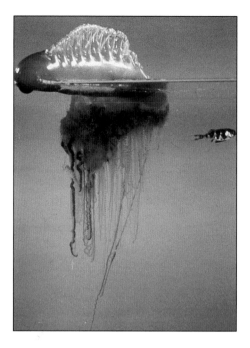

Fig. 3-6. **Atlantic Portuguese-Man-O-War,** *Physalia physalis* (Linnaeus). This species is found in the tropical Atlantic and throughout the West Indies. Attains a length of 33 centimeters (13 inches) or more, and tentacles may hang down into the water for a distance of more than 30.1 meters (33 yards). Courtesy of Miami Seaquarium.

deceive you—they are painful to touch. Found throughout the Indo-Pacific region, the height of the colony is about 20.3 centimeters (8 inches). Closely related species inhabit the West Indies.

FAMILY PHYSALIIDAE

ATLANTIC PORTUGUESE-MAN-O-WAR or BLUE BOTTLE, *Physalia physalis* (Linnaeus) (fig. 3-6). This particular species inhabits the tropical Atlantic, ranging as far north as the Bay of Fundy, the Hebrides, and the Mediterranean Sea and attains a length of 33 centimeters (13 inches) or more. This hydroid is most commonly mistaken for a true jellyfish. Actually, it is a colonial hydroid. It is almost always found floating at the surface of the water. Suspended from the balloonlike floats are the stinging tentacles which may trail several feet down into the water. Figure 3-7 shows the sting inflicted by this Atlantic Portuguese-Man-O-War, which is very painful. Fatalities have been reported.

INDO-PACIFIC PORTUGUESE-MAN-O-WAR, *Physalia utriculus* (La Martinière)(fig. 3-8). Inhabits the tropical Indo-Pacific region. Attains a length of 12.7 centimeters (5 inches), and tentacles may hang down a distance of 11.8 meters (13 yards). Capable of inflicting extremely painful stings. May be fatal.

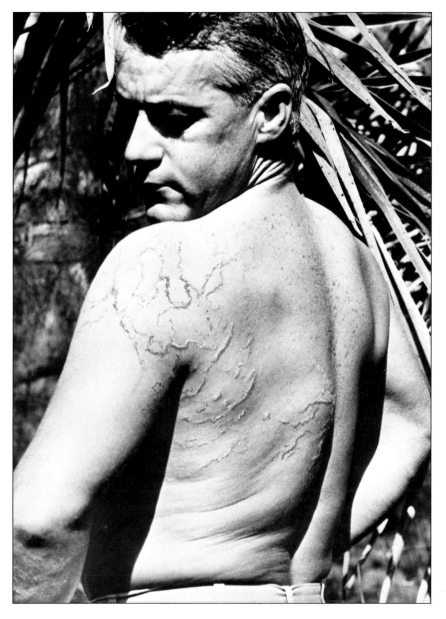

Fig. 3-7. Sting inflicted by the **Atlantic Portuguese-Man-O-War**, *Physalia physalis* (Linnaeus). The sting caused intense pain, resulting in severe respiratory distress, and muscular paralysis, which almost caused the victim to drown. The pain lasted for about five hours and the scars for about a year. Courtesy of R. Straughan.

Fig. 3-8. **Indo-Pacific Portuguese-Man-O-War**, *Physalia utriculus* (La Martinière). This smaller species is found throughout the tropical Indo-Pacific region. Attains a length of 12.7 centimeters (5 inches), and tentacles may hang down a distance of 11.8 meters (13 yards). Both species are capable of inflicting extremely painful stings. Painting by M. Shirao.

JELLYFISHES, SCYPHOZOA

This class includes the larger medusae, having eight notches in the margin of the bell. It is estimated that there are about two hundred species of jellyfish capable of stinging and producing mild skin irritations, but only a few might be considered especially dangerous. These include:

FAMILY CHIRODROPIDAE

DEADLY SEA WASP or BOX JELLY, *Chironex fleckeri* Southcott (fig. 3-9). This is one of the most deadly stinging creatures in the sea. The bell may reach 11.4 centimeters (4.5 inches) in height. It is the cause of numerous deaths along the north Queensland coast of Australia. *Chironex* is capable of inflicting a severely lacerated rash and excruciating pain. Due to circulatory failure and respiratory paralysis, death may take place within a few minutes. An antivenin has now been produced for use against envenomation by this jellyfish. The anitvenin is available through the Commonwealth Serum Laboratories, Melbourne, Australia. A vaccine for preventive measures is in preparation.

Fig. 3-9. **Deadly Sea Wasp,** *Chironex fleckeri* Southcott. One of the most deadly stinging creatures in the sea. Living specimen taken in an aquarium, Cairns, Queensland, Australia. Specimen about 7.6 centimeters (3 inches) across the bell. Courtesy of Keith Gillett.

FAMILY CARYBDEIDAE

SEA WASP, *Carybdea alata* Reynaud (fig. 3-10). This species inhabits the tropical Pacific, Atlantic, and Indian Oceans. Can produce painful stings.

FAMILY CHIRODROPIDAE

SEA WASP, *Chiropsalmus quadrigatus* Haeckel (fig. 3-11). This stinging jellyfish is an inhabitant of northern Australia, the Philippines, and the Indian Ocean. The species is sometimes confused with *Chironex,* which is much more dangerous. A closely related species occurs in the Atlantic.

FAMILY CYANEIDAE

SEA BLUBBER or LION'S MANE, *Cyanea capillata* Eschscholtz (fig. 3-12). The sea blubber inhabits the North Atlantic and Pacific, the southern coast of New England to the Arctic Ocean, France to northern Russia, and the Baltic Sea, Alaska to Puget Sound, Japan and China. Other stinging species of this genus are found in the tropical and temperate Pacific Ocean. They may attain large size. Large specimens have measured more than 1.5 meters (5 feet) across the bell, length of tentacles 73 meters (240 feet).

Fig. 3-10, *left*. **Sea Wasp**, *Carybdea alata* Reynaud. This sea wasp is able to inflict a painful sting, but is not as dangerous as *Chironex fleckeri*. Photo of living specimen taken in an aquarium. Specimen measured about 10.1 centimeters (4 inches) across the bell. Courtesy of Paul Humann. Fig. 3-11, *right*. **Sea Wasp**, *Chiropsalmus quadrigatus* Haeckel. This species can also inflict a very painful sting, but is not as dangerous as *Chironex fleckeri*, with which it is sometimes confused. Specimen measured about 3.5 centimeters (1.4 inches) across the bell. Photo taken in an aquarium at Cairns, Queensland, Australia. Courtesy of Charles Arneson.

SEA ANEMONES and CORALS, ANTHOZOA
FAMILY ACROPORIDAE

ELK HORN CORAL, *Acropora palmata* (Lamarck)(figs. 3-13 and 3-14). Inhabits Florida Keys, Bahamas, and West Indies.

FAMILY ACTINIIDAE

SEA ANEMONE, *Actinia equina* Linnaeus (fig. 3-15). Inhabits the eastern Atlantic from the Arctic Ocean to the Gulf of Guinea, the Mediterranean Sea, the Black Sea, and the Sea of Azov. Can inflict a painful sting.

SEA ANEMONE, *Anemonia sulcata* (Pennant)(fig. 3-15). Inhabits the Eastern Atlantic, from Norway and Scotland to the Canaries, and the Mediterranean Sea.

Fig. 3-12. **Sea Blubber**, *Cyanea capillata* Eschscholtz. This is the largest of the jelly-fishes and allegedly may attain a diameter across the bell of more than 1.5 meters (5 feet) with the tentacles dangling down more than 73 meters (240 feet). Courtesy of Ron and Valerie Taylor.

Fig. 3-13. **Elk Horn Coral**, *Acropora palmata* (Lamarck). Large branch measuring about 45.7 centimeters (18 inches) in height. W.L.R.I. photo.

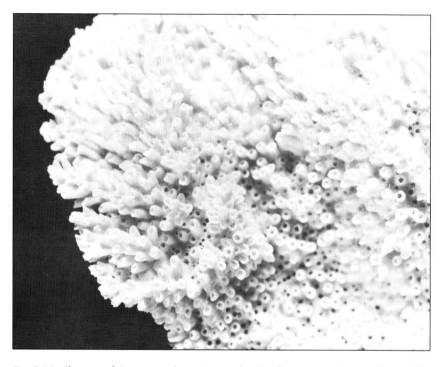

Fig. 3-14. Close-up of *Acropora palmata* (Lamarck). Corals are razor-sharp and can inflict wounds which at first may appear to be insignificant, but in the tropics are slow to heal and may result in serious infections. Size variable. Courtesy Smithsonian Institution.

FAMILY ACTINODENDRONIDAE

HELL'S FIRE SEA ANEMONE, *Actinodendron plumosum* Haddon (fig. 3-16). This sea anemone is usually found on the shady side of rocks or under coral ledges, but seldom in the sand. The hell's fire sea anemone ranges in size from 15.2 centimeters (6 inches) to 30.4 centimeters (12 inches). When the sea anemone is extended, it takes on a flowerlike appearance, but when in the contracted state, it has been described as appearing to have a "top hat." It can inflict serious and extremely painful stings. It may produce ulceration at the envenomation site and severe systemic effects, such as chills, fever, gastrointestinal upset, extreme thirst, and prostration. It is very slow to heal.

FAMILY ALICIIDAE

SEA ANEMONE, *Triactis producta* Klunzinger (fig. 3-17). This is one of the more dangerous of the sea anemones, and can inflict an extremely painful

Fig. 3-15. *Top left*, **Sea Anemone**, *Actinia equina* Linnaeus. Diameter up to 20 centimeters (7.9 inches). *Top right*, **Sea Anemone**, *Anemonia sulcata* (Pennant). Diameter up to 7 centimeters (2.5 inches). *Bottom left*, **Sea Anemone**, *Adamsia palliata* (Bohadsch). Diameter up to 4 centimeters (1.5 inches). *Bottom right*, **Sea Anemone**, *Sagartia elegans* (Dalyell). Diameter up to 8 centimeters (3 inches). All of these anemones are capable of inflicting painful stings. Drawing by H. Baerg.

Fig. 3-16. **Hell's Fire Anemone**, *Actinodendron plumosum* Haddon. Wounds inflicted by this sea anemone usually become ulcerated and may take several months to heal. Photo taken in Guam. Courtesy of R.F. Myers.

Fig. 3-17. **Sea Anemone**, *Triactis producta* Klunzinger. This Red Sea sea anemone, despite its small size, can inflict an extremely painful sting. Photo taken at night in the Eilat, Gulf of Aqaba, Egypt. Courtesy of David Masry.

sting. It inhabits the Red Sea. Its diameter is about 4.1 centimeters (1.6 inches), and when fully extended it attains a height of about 7.6 centimeters (3 inches).

FAMILY HORMATHIIDAE

SEA ANEMONE, *Adamsia palliata* (Bohadsch) (fig. 3-15). Ranges from Norway to Spain, and to the Mediterranean Sea. Can inflict a painful sting.

FAMILY SAGARTIIDAE

ROSY ANEMONE, *Sagartia elegans* (Dalyell) (fig. 3-15). Ranges from Iceland to the Atlantic coast of France, the Mediterranean Sea, and the coast of Africa. Can inflict a painful sting. Diameter 8 centimeters (3.2 inches).

Venom Apparatus of Coelenterates: The venom apparatus of coelenterates consists of the nematocysts or stinging cells, which are located largely on the tentacles (fig. 3-18). These nematocysts are situated within the outer layer of the tissue of the tentacle. Each of the capsulelike nematocysts is contained inside a capsulelike device called the cnidoblast. Projecting at one point on the outer surface of the cnidoblast is the triggerlike cnidocil. Not all species possess a cnidocil. Some may be equipped with special chemoreceptors which are able to detect food and thereby activate the nematocyst.

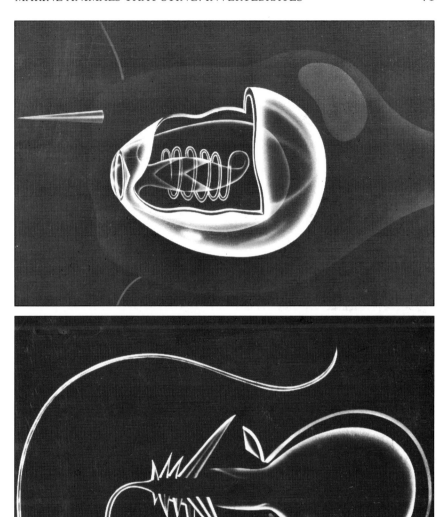

Fig. 3-18. Nematocyst or stinging apparatus of coelenterates. *Top*, undischarged nematocyst. Note the coiled threadlike tube which conveys the venom. Semidiagrammatic. *Bottom*, discharged nematocyst. Drawing by Robert Kreuzinger.

Contained within the fluid-filled capsular nematocyst is a hollow, coiled, thread tube. The opening through which the thread tube is everted is closed prior to discharge by a lidlike device called the operculum. The fluid within the capsule is the venom. Stimulation of the cnidocil or chemoreceptor appears to produce a change in the capsular wall of the nematocyst causing the operculum to spring open like a trap door, and the thread tube conveying the venom is everted (fig. 3-19). The sharp tip of the thread tube penetrates the skin of the victim and the venom is thereby injected. When a diver comes in contact with the tentacles of a coelenterate, he brushes up against thousands of these minute stinging nematocysts.

Medical Aspects: The symptoms produced by coelenterate stings vary according to the species, the site of the sting, and the person. In general, those caused by hydroids and hydroid corals (*Millepora*) are primarily local skin irritations. *Physalia* stings may be very painful (figs. 3-20 through 3-27). Sea anemones and true corals produce a similar reaction, but may be

Fig. 3-19. Photomicrographs of nematocysts: *Left*, nematocysts of the **Portuguese-Man-O-War**, *Physalia utriculus*. Undischarged and discharged nematocysts of both the small and large sizes are seen (Approx. ×290). Courtesy of C.E. Lane. *Right*, nematocysts of the **Sea Wasp**, *Chironex fleckeri* Southcott. The large undischarged nematocysts are the ones believed to be the most dangerous to man. (Approx. ×240). Courtesy of J.H. Barnes.

Fig. 3-20, *left*. Hydroid sting from an unidentified species. Right upper arm. Taken at Culebra Island, Puerto Rico. Courtesy of R. M. Mandojana. Fig. 3-21, *right*. **Fire coral** stings occurred on the buttocks when heavy surf rolled the diver over the reef. Taken at Culebra Island, Puerto Rico. Identification of fire coral unknown. Courtesy of R.M. Mandojana.

accompanied by general symptoms. Ulcerations of the skin may be quite severe in lesions produced by *Sagartia* and *Actinodendron*. Symptoms resulting from scyphozoans vary greatly. The sting of some scyphozoans is too mild to be noticeable, whereas *Chironex, Cyanea,* and *Chiropsalmus* are capable of inflicting very painful local and generalized symptoms. *Chironex* is one of the most venomous marine organisms known and may produce death within a few minutes. The venomous properties of a coelenterate sting depend not only upon the chemical composition of the venom, but also upon the ability of the nematocyst to penetrate the skin of the victim.

Symptoms most commonly encountered vary from an immediate mild prickly or stinging sensation like that of a nettle sting, to a burning, throbbing, or shooting pain which may render the victim unconscious. In some cases, the pain is restricted to an area within the immediate vicinity of the contact, or it may radiate to the groin, abdomen, or armpit. The area coming in contact with the tentacles usually becomes reddened. This is followed by a severe inflammatory rash, blistering, swelling, minute skin hemorrhages, and possible ulcerations. In severe cases, in addition to shock, there may be

Fig. 3-22. *Left*, enlarged view of one of the branches of *Lytocarpus nuttingi*, which bears the polyps and stinging nematocysts. *Right*, photomicrograph of the nematotheca of *Lytocarpus nuttingi* with several discharged and undischarged nematocysts inside, and one discharged nematocyst outside of the nematotheca (right of center). The base of the nematocyst contains the venom. Courtesy of R. Given.

Fig. 3-23. Wound on left wrist produced by *T. producta*. Initial contact caused a burning or stinging sensation, followed by swelling at the sting site and then of the entire arm. The pain became increasingly intense, followed by numbness. There was no ulceration (although ulceration may occur), and the lesion gradually healed in about six weeks. Courtesy of D. Masry.

Fig. 3-24, *left*. Upper right leg of U.S. Air Force airman who was stung by *Actinodendron* while swimming in Cam Ranh Bay, South Vietnam. Inital symptoms consisted of a mild stinging sensation, which became progressively worse; later the area became swollen and the skin broke down into numerous small ulcerations, which healed slowly over a period of several weeks. Courtesy of P.A. Hansen. Fig. 3-25, *right*. *Chiropsalmus* sting on the knee. Cairns, Australia. Courtesy of J.H. Barnes.

muscular cramps, abdominal rigidity, diminished touch and temperature sensation, nausea, vomiting, severe backache, loss of speech, frothing at the mouth, the sensation of constriction of the throat, respiratory difficulty, paralysis, delirium, convulsions, and death.

    Treatment: Treatment must be directed toward accomplishing three objectives: relieving pain, alleviating effects of the poison, and controlling primary shock. Morphine is effective in relieving pain. Intravenous injections of calcium gluconate have been recommended for the control of muscular spasms. Oral antihistamines and topical cream are useful in treating the rash. Diluted ammonium hydroxide, sodium bicarbonate, olive oil, sugar, ethyl alcohol, and other types of soothing lotions have been used with varying degrees of success. Papain (meat tenderizer) has been used with some success in the treatment of jellyfish stings. Prompt application of methyl, ethyl alcohol, or vinegar has been found to be effective in stopping

Fig. 3-26. Near fatal sting by *Chironex fleckeri* on a thirteen-year-old boy at Cairns, Australia. The boy's life was saved by flooding his skin immediately with rubbing alcohol. Vinegar is said to be even more effective. Courtesy of J.H. Barnes.

Fig. 3-27. Photograph of the arm of a four-year-old boy fatally stung by *Chironex fleckeri,* near Cairns, Queensland, Australia, January 31, 1966. The child was being supported by his father in waist-deep water near the beach at the time of stinging. Child died within thirty-five minutes of being stung. Courtesy of J. Barnes.

envenomation by nematocysts. Keep in mind that as long as the tentacle of the jellyfish remains in contact with the skin, the nematocysts will continue to discharge their venom. It is therefore important to remove or inactivate the nematocysts as rapidly as possible. Thus the immediate application of vinegar to the skin has been found to be very effective in reducing the severity of the envenomation. Be careful about removing the tentacles with your bare fingers as further envenomation will take place. Use a stick, sand, cloth, or seaweed to remove the tentacles only after the application of alcohol or vinegar. Artificial respiration, cardiac and respiratory stimulants, and other forms of supportive measures may be required. The only antivenin generally available for any coelenterate envenomation for treatment of the *Chironex fleckeri* is produced by the Commonwealth Serum Laboratories, Melbourne, Australia. It may be useful in treating other types of coelenterate stings, because the venom of many species appear to be chemically similar in composition.

Prevention: It is important to bear in mind that the tentacles of some species of jellyfish may trail a great distance from the body of the animal—as much as 50 feet or more, in some instances. Consequently, underwear or rubber skin diving suits are useful in affording protection from attacks from these creatures. Divers working in tropical waters should be completely clothed. Even though appearing dead, jellyfish washed up on the beach may be quite capable of inflicting a serious sting. The tentacles of some jellyfish may cling to the skin. Care should be exercised in the removal of the tentacles, or additional stings may result. Do not use a towel, rag, seaweed, stick, or handful of sand to remove tentacles until alcohol or vinegar is applied. Swimming soon after a storm in tropical waters in which large numbers of jellyfish were previously present may result in multiple severe stings from remnants of damaged tentacles floating in the water. Upon being stung, the victim should make every effort to get out of the water as quickly as possible because of the danger of drowning. Diluted ammonia and alcohol or vinegar should be applied to the site of the stings as soon as possible. Rubbing the body with mineral oil or baby oil may help to prevent stings to some extent.

CORAL CUTS

The problem of coral cuts is deserving of special mention, since they represent an ever-present annoyance to the diver working in tropical areas. Despite their delicate appearance, stony corals have calcareous outer skeletons with razor-sharp edges that are capable of inflicting nasty wounds. The severity of coral cuts is probably due to a combination of factors: mechanical laceration of the skin by the razorsharp exoskeleton of the coral; envenomation to some extent by the nematocysts when inflicted by a living coral; introduction of foreign material into the wound (calcium carbonate, sand, debris); secondary bacterial infection; and climatic conditions (high temperature and humidity) suitable for bacterial growth. The injuries are generally superficial, but are notoriously slow in healing, and often cause temporary disability. When working in tropical reef areas for extended periods of time, "minor" coral cuts can rapidly become major medical problems, frequently resulting in severe cellulitis. Consequently, coral cuts, no matter how small, must not be ignored.

Treatment: Prompt cleansing of the wound, removal of foreign particles and dead tissue, and the application of antiseptic agents are recommended. A brief rinse with acetic acid 5 percent (vinegar) or isopropyl alcohol 40 to 70 percent usually diminishes the discomfort. In severe cases, it may be necessary to prescribe bed rest for the patient, with elevation of the limb, kaolin poultices, magnesium sulfate in glycerin solution dressings, aloe cream, and antibiotics. Antihistaminic drugs given orally, or applied locally to the wound, afford relief of pain.

Prevention: When working in the vicinity of corals, take every precaution to avoid contact with them. Do not handle corals with bare hands. Wear leather or heavy cotton gloves, and rubber-soled canvas shoes, or a completely-soled flipper.

CONE SHELLS, OCTOPUSES, ETC.—MOLLUSCA

Stinging or venomous molluscs of concern to the skin diver fall largely into two classes:

1. Gastropoda or univalve molluscs.
2. Cephalopoda—octopuses and squids.

First we will consider the individual snails and cone shells (Gastropoda).

FAMILY CONIDAE

The univalves include land, freshwater, and marine snails and slugs. Members of this class are characterized by a single shell, or lack of a shell. The body is usually asymmetrical in a spirally coiled shell (the slugs are an exception to this arrangement). Typically, there is a distinct head, with one to two pairs of tentacles, two eyes, and a large flattened, fleshy foot. Only members of the genus *Conus* are of particular concern to the skin diver.

Univalve molluscs of the genus *Conus,* or cone shells, as they are commonly called, because of their conelike shape, are favorites of shell collectors because of their ornate and attractive patterns. There are more than four hundred species of cone shells, and all of them contain a highly developed venom apparatus. Cone shells are usually found under rocks, coral, or crawling along the sand. Several of the tropical species have caused deaths. Some of the more dangerous species are listed below.

COURT CONE, *Conus aulicus* Linnaeus (fig. 3-28). Ranges from Polynesia westward to the Indian Ocean.

GEOGRAPHIC CONE, *Conus geographus* Linnaeus (fig. 3-29). Inhabits the Indo-Pacific, from Polynesia to east Africa.

MARBLED CONE, *Conus marmoreus* Linnaeus (fig. 3-30). Ranges from Polynesia westward to the Indian Ocean.

STRIATED CONE, *Conus striatus* Linnaeus (fig. 3-31). Inhabits the Indo-Pacific, from Australia to east Africa.

TEXTILE CONE, *Conus textile* Linnaeus (fig. 3-32). Ranges from Polynesia to the Red Sea.

TULIP CONE, *Conus tulipa* Linnaeus (fig. 3-33). Ranges from Polynesia to the Red Sea.

Venom Apparatus of Cone Shells: The venom apparatus consists of the venom bulb, venom duct, radular sheath, and radular teeth (fig. 3-34). The pharynx and proboscis, which are a part of the digestive system, also play an important role as accessory organs. The venom apparatus lies in a cavity within the animal. It is believed that preparatory to stinging, the radular teeth, which are housed in the radular sheath, are released into the pharynx, and thence to the proboscis, where they are grasped for thrusting into the flesh of the victim. The venom, believed to be produced in the venom duct, is probably forced under pressure by contraction of the venom bulb and duct into the radular sheath, and thereby forced into the coiled radular teeth (fig. 3-35).

Medical Aspects: Stings produced by *Conus* are of the puncture wound variety. Localized ischemia, cyanosis, numbness in the area about the wound, or a sharp stinging or burning sensation are usually the initial symptoms.

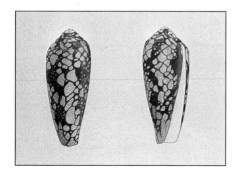

Fig. 3-28. **Court Cone,** *Conus aulicus* Linnaeus. Length 14.9 centimeters (5.9 inches). Drawing by S. Arita.

Fig. 3-29. **Geographic Cone**, *Conus geographus* Linnaeus. This species has caused more fatalities among humans than any other member of this group. Attains a length of 12.7 centimeters (5 inches). Courtesy of D. Faulkner.

Fig. 3-30. **Marbled Cone**, *Conus marmoreus* Linnaeus. This cone has inflicted stings in humans, but no fatalities. Attains a length of 10.1 centimeters (4 inches). Courtesy of Ron and Valerie Taylor.

Fig. 3-31. **Striated Cone,** *Conus striatus* Linnaeus. Length 10 centimeters (3.9 inches). (From Hiyama).

Fig. 3-32. **Textile Cone,** *Conus textile* Linnaeus. Length 10 centimeters (3.9 inches). (From Hiyama).

Numbness and tingling begin at the wound site and may spread rapidly, involving the entire body, but are particularly pronounced about the lips and mouth. In severe cases, paralysis may be present. Respiratory distress is usually absent. Coma may ensue, and death is said to be the result of cardiac failure. The clinical condition of the patient may get worse during the first six hours after being bitten. If the victim survives, he usually recovers within

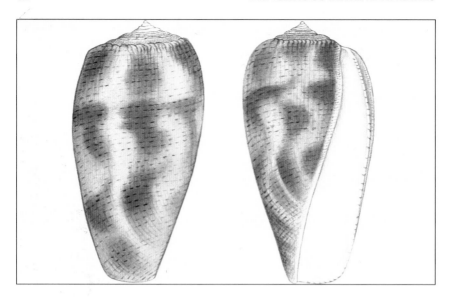

Fig. 3-33. **Tulip Cone**, *Conus tulipa* Linnaeus. Length 7.5 centimeters (2.9 inches). (From Hiyama).

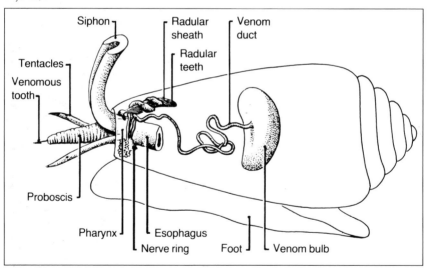

Fig. 3-34. Venom apparatus of the cone shell. Drawing by R.H. Knabenbauer.

Fig. 3-35. *Top*, photomicrograph of the harpoonlike tip of the radular tooth of *Conus striatus*. *Center*, radular tooth of *Conus striatus*. *Bottom*, semidiagrammatic drawing of a typical radular tooth of *Conus*. The radular teeth are composed of a flat sheet of chitin rolled into a tubelike structure. The venom is contained within the lumen of the tooth. Upper picture illustrates base of tooth attached to ligament. Barbed tip of hollow tooth in lower drawing. Drawing by R. Kreuzinger.

a period of twenty-four hours. The localized reaction may persist for several weeks.

Treatment: Cone shell stings should be treated like a snake bite, with a ligature, incision, and removal of the venom by suction. Incision and suction are of little value if more than one hour has lapsed after the wound was inflicted. The patient should rest as much as possible and be moved to a hospital as soon as possible. Respiratory distress may develop, requiring immediate mouth-to-mouth resuscitation until the patient can be transferred to a mechanical respirator. External cardiac massage may be needed if pulse and heartbeat are absent. If the patient is in a state of shock, place him on his back so that his head is lower than his feet.

When the patient arrives at the hospital, cardiac massage, defibrillation, vasopressor drugs, etc., may be required. Respiratory depressants should be avoided, and respiratory stimulants are probably useless because of the neuromuscular blocking action of the cone shell venom. Unfortunately, there are no specific antivenins available for cone shell envenomations.

Prevention: Live cone shells should be handled with care, and effort should be made to avoid coming in contact with the soft parts of the animal. Do not place cone shells in pockets. They are capable of inflicting stings through clothing.

OCTOPUSES, SQUIDS, ETC.—CEPHALOPODA
FAMILY OCTOPODIDAE

This group includes the nautilus, squid, cuttlefish, and octopus. The head is large and contains conspicuous and well-developed eyes. The mouth, armed with horny jaws and a radula, is surrounded by eight or ten tentacles equipped with numerous suckers or hooks. Rapid movements can be produced by expelling water from the mantle cavity through the siphon.

Few marine animals have received greater attention from fiction writers than the octopus. Truly, it is a remarkable creature, but most species are grossly overrated as a hazard to the diver. Both curious and cautious, the octopus can hardly be considered the demon of the seas many writers make it out to be. Large specimens may exceed 7.6 meters (25 feet) (fig. 3-36) in span, but those encountered at diving depths are generally smaller. The giant squid that is commonly taken off the coast of South America may attain several times the length of the largest octopus, but is for the most part a deep-water inhabitant, and of little concern to skin divers. The nautilus and

Fig. 3-36. *Octopus apollyon* Berry. Courtesy of F. Bavendam.

cuttlefish are not considered to be of medical importance. Octopuses tend to hide in holes or underwater caves. Areas such as these should be avoided by the inexperienced diver. There is a remote danger that a diver may be trapped underwater when entering a cave, even by a relatively small specimen, if it can get a good grip on a smooth surface of the diver. A more practical danger comes from the careless handling of small specimens of octopuses, since these animals possess a well-developed venom apparatus and produce their injurious effects by biting.

Cephalopods can be identified only with difficulty by specialists. However, one species that does bear particular mention is the Australian blue-ringed octopus, *Octopus maculosus* Hoyle (fig. 3-37), and the closely related species *Octopus lunulatus* Quoy and Gaimard. Its length is about 20.3 centimeters (8 inches). Both species are venomous and capable of causing death. They are Indo-Pacific species, especially common along Southern Australian coasts, but *Octopus lunulatus* appears to have a more northerly distribution.

Venom Apparatus of the Octopus: The venom apparatus of the octopus is composed of the so-called anterior and posterior salivary glands, the salivary ducts, the buccal mass, and the jaws, or beak (fig. 3-38). The mouth of the octopus is situated in the center of the oral and anterior surface of the

Fig. 3-37. *Octopus maculosus* Hoyle. Courtesy of Cousteau Society.

arms, surrounded by a circular lip, fringed with fingerlike papillae (fig. 3-39). The mouth leads into a pharyngeal cavity having thick muscular walls. This entire muscular complex is known as the buccal mass, which is surrounded and concealed by the muscular bases of the arms. The buccal mass is furnished with two powerful dorsal and ventral chitinous jaws, whose shape resembles that of a parrot's beak. The arrangement of the jaws differs from the parrot in that the ventral one bites outside of the dorsal and is wider and larger. These jaws are able to bite vertically with great force, tearing the captured food which is held by the suckers before it is passed on to the rasping action of the radula. The duct from the posterior salivary glands opens on the tip of the subradular organ, which appears as an outgrowth in front of the tongue. The paired ducts from the anterior glands open into the pharynx laterally and posteriorly. The venom is discharged from these ducts into the pharynx.

Medical Aspects: Octopus bites usually consist of two small puncture wounds which are produced by the sharp parrotlike chitinous jaws (fig. 3-40). A burning or tingling sensation is the usual initial symptom. At first, the discomfort is localized, but may later radiate to include the entire appendage. Bleeding is frequently profuse for the size of the bite, which may indicate that the clotting process of the blood is retarded. Swelling, redness, and heat commonly develop in the area about the wound. Recovery is

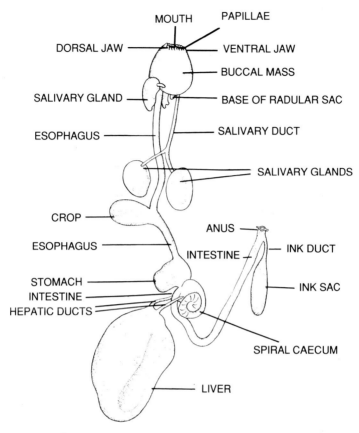

Fig. 3-38. Anatomy of the venom apparatus of the octopus. Drawing by R. Kreuzinger.

generally uneventful. However, bites from the Australian blue-ringed octopus can be serious. Initially, the bite may be painless. Within a few minutes
the area about the bite appears blanched and soon becomes swollen and
hemorrhagic. A stinging sensation may develop shortly thereafter. The
venom (maculotoxin) is a potent neurotoxin causing a sensation of numbness and tingling around the mouth, neck, and head. This may be followed
by nausea and vomiting. In severe envenomations respiratory distress soon
develops, followed by visual disturbances, ocular paralysis, dizziness, difficulty in speech and swallowing, lack of motor coordination, muscular
weakness and, possibly, complete paralysis. In fatal cases, the patient loses
consciousness, and death is due to a respiratory paralysis. If the patient
survives, the duration of the paralysis is about four to twelve hours.

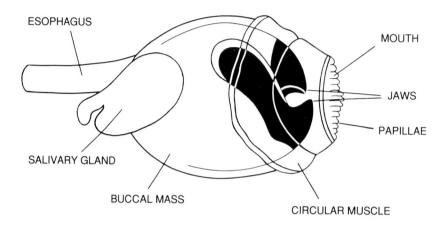

ESOPHAGUS

MOUTH

JAWS

PAPILLAE

SALIVARY GLAND

BUCCAL MASS

CIRCULAR MUSCLE

Fig. 3-39. Buccal mass of an octopus showing the mouth and jaws. Drawing by R. Kreuzinger.

Fig. 3-40. Octopus bites believed to have been inflicted by *O. apollyon*. The bites took place while removing the animal from an aquarium at the Marine Science Center, Oregon State University, Newport, Oregon. The bite is similar to that of a bee sting, with profuse bleeding from the wound, redness, swelling, and healing in about ten days. Courtesy of R. Hildebrand.

Several fatalities have been reported from octopus bites. The following report is one such example. The incident took place near East Point, Darwin, Australia. According to the account, a diver captured a small blue-ringed octopus (probably *Octopus lunulatus*), which had a span of about 19.8

centimeters (7.8 inches). The diver permitted the octopus to crawl over his arms and shoulders, and finally to the back of his neck, where the animal remained for a few moments. During the period that the octopus was on his neck, a small bite was inflicted, producing a trickle of blood. A few minutes after the bite, the victim complained of a sensation of dryness in his mouth and of difficulty in swallowing. After walking a short distance up the beach from the scene of the accident, the victim began to vomit, developed a loss of muscular control, and finally suffered from respiratory distress, and was unable to speak. Even though he was rushed to a hospital and placed on a respirator, the victim expired about two hours after being bitten.

Treatment: Octopus bites from most species are usually of minor concern and can be treated symptomatically. Bites from the blue-ringed octopus must be treated vigorously. Ligature, when possible, and removal of the venom by suction, or washing out of the wound should be performed promptly. The patient should be placed at rest and given reassurance. If respiratory paralysis develops, mouth-to-mouth resuscitation and cardiac massage may be required. Attention must be given to clearing the airway of the patient from vomitus (laying the patient on his side is helpful). The head of the patient should be extended backwards as far as it will go and the jaw lifted forward, bringing the lower teeth in front of the upper teeth. This procedure will help to pull the tongue away from the back of the throat. The victim should be transported to the hospital as soon as possible. Central respiratory stimulants may be of value, especially during the recovery phase. The administration of artificial respiration is of the utmost importance. There is no specific antivenin available.

Prevention: Underwater caves which are likely to be inhabited by octopuses should be avoided by the inexperienced diver. The wearing of an outer cloth garment makes it difficult for an octopus to adhere to the skin. Regardless of their size, octopuses should be handled with gloves. Some of the smaller species seem to be the most aggressive biters. If not familiar with the species, it is best to leave it alone. Stabbing deep between the eyes is the method of choice for killing an octopus.

SEGMENTED WORMS, ANNELIDA

Segmented worms, or annelids, are organisms having an elongate body, which is usually segmented, each segment having paired setae, or bristlelike structures. In some species these setae are developed into a stinging mechanism. Still other species have tough chitinous jaws with which they can inflict a painful bite. Annelid worms are usually encountered when turning over rocks or coral boulders.

There are many species of annelid worms which might be listed, but the following species are representatives of the two types: (1) those having biting jaws (*Glycera, Eunice*) and (2) those having stinging setae (*Eurythöe, Hermodice*).

FAMILY AMPHINOMIDAE

BITING REEF WORM, *Eunice aphroditois* (Pallas) (figs. 3-41 to 3-43). Circumtropical in distribution.

BRISTLEWORM, *Eurythöe complanata* (Pallas) (fig. 3-44). Found in the Gulf of Mexico and throughout the tropical Pacific.

BRISTLEWORM, *Hermodice carunculata* (Pallas) (fig. 3-45). Inhabits the Gulf of Mexico.

FAMILY GLYCERIDAE

BLOODWORM, *Glycera dibranchiata* Ehlers (fig. 3-46). Found along the coast of North Carolina to northeast Canada.

Medical Aspects: The chitinous jaws of *Glycera* are able to penetrate the skin and to produce a painful sensation similar to that of a bee sting (fig. 3-47). The marks from the jaws are oval-shaped, and are about as large as

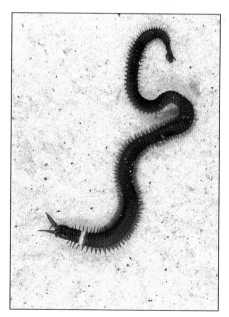

Fig. 3-41. **Biting Reef Worm,** *Eunice aphroditois* (Pallas). Adult worm. Length 150 centimeters (59.1 inches). Photo by Keith Gillett.

Fig. 3-42. Enlarged view of ventral side of head showing biting jaws. Photo by Keith Gillett.

Fig. 3-43. Skin removed from lower jaw to reveal biting jaws. This worm is suspected of having venomous jaws and can inflict a painful bite. Attains a length of more than 150 centimeters (59.1 inches). Photo by Keith Gillett.

the inner circle of the following letter "O," in the center of which is a small reddish spot usually indicating where the jaws have pierced the skin, and bordered by a surrounding area of blanching. The wounded area may become hot and swollen, and may remain so for a day or two. The swelling may be followed by numbness and itching.

Contact with the setae or bristles of the bristleworm may produce inflammation, intense itching, swelling, and numbness, which may persist

Fig. 3-44, *left*. **Bristleworm**, *Eurythöe complanata* (Pallas). Courtesy of A. Bruce Bowker, Aquaventure, Bonaire, N.A. Fig. 3-45, *right*. **Bristleworm**, *Hermodice carunculata* (Pallas). This species is said to be one of the most dangerous of the bristleworms. Its length is 29.7 centimeters (11.7 inches). Courtesy of Ron and Nancy Sefton.

for several days. The numbness may persist for weeks. It is not definitely known whether a toxin is actually involved. *Eunice aphroditois* (Pallas) may attain a length of 1.5 meters (5 feet) and is equipped with large chitinous jaws that are capable of inflicting a nasty bite. The wounds may be a few millimeters in diameter, soon becoming swollen, hot, and inflamed. These wounds can become infected.

Treatment: The treatment of bristleworm stings is largely symptomatic. The bristles can best be removed by applying adhesive tape to them, or by rubbing the area with sand. The topical application of alcohol or soothing lotions may be helpful, and local anesthetic creams, ointments, or sprays are useful. Steroid creams, antihistamines, and antibiotics may be required.

Prevention: Exercise care in the handling of noxious annelid worms. Cotton gloves will probably provide adequate protection from bloodworms, but rubber or heavy leather gloves are advisable when handling bristle-worms.

STARFISHES, SEA URCHINS, SEA CUCUMBERS— ECHINODERMATA

Echinoderms are characterized by having radial symmetry, with the body usually of five radii around an oral-suboral axis, comprised of calcareous plates which form a more or less rigid skeleton, or with plates and spicules embedded in the body wall. Starfishes or sea stars, sea cucumbers, and sea urchins are all members of this group.

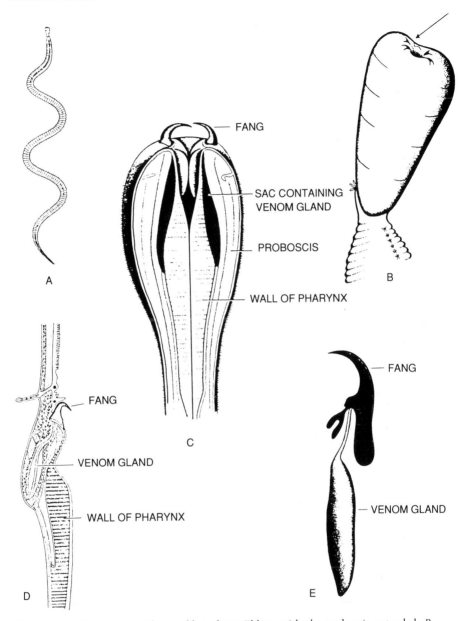

Fig. 3-46. A. **Bloodworm**, *Glycera dibranchiata* Ehlers, with the proboscis extended. *B.* Enlargement of proboscis of *Glycera* showing the fangs at tip of arrow. *C.* Longitudinal section of the extended proboscis of *Glycera* showing the venomous fangs and related structures. *D.* Longitudinal section through a portion of the pharynx and proboscis in the retracted position showing the anatomical relationships of the venom apparatus. *E.* Fang and venom gland removed from the proboscis of *Glycera*. Drawing by R. Kreuzinger, after Ehlers.

Fig. 3-47. **Bloodworm**, *Glycera dibranchiata* Ehlers. These worms are used extensively in the United States and Canada as bait worms. When handled, they will sometimes bite. They attain a length of 35.5 centimeters (14 inches). Looking into the jaws, the four dark lines are the fangs. Taken from movie film, courtesy of P. Saunders.

FAMILY ACANTHASTERIDAE

THE CROWN OF THORNS STARFISH, *Acanthaster planci* (Linnaeus) (fig. 3-48) developed its greatest notoriety because of its massive infestations and destruction of some of the coral reefs in the Indo-Pacific region. The starfish possesses thirteen to sixteen arms or rays, and may be more than 60.9 centimeters (24 inches) in diameter. The upper surface of the starfish is covered with numerous long, sharp, stout spines, attaining a length of 7.1 centimeters (2.8 inches) or more. The spines are covered by a thick integumentary sheath which secretes the venom. These spines can inflict painful wounds. Despite the stout appearance of the spines, they are friable and may break off in the wound.

Medical Aspects: Contact with the spines of the venomous starfish may cause extremely painful wounds accompanied by redness, swelling, numbness, and possible paralysis. Nausea and vomiting may be present and the wound may become infected. Some persons are sensitive to the slime of this starfish and contact with the slime may cause a dermatitis.

Treatment: Spines are sometimes embedded and may have to be surgically removed. Exposure of the wound to the suction pads of a living starfish

Fig. 3-48. **Crown of Thorns Starfish**, *Acanthaster planci* (Linnaeus). Spines may attain a length of 6 centimeters (2.5 inches) or more, and the starfish more than 60 centimeters (24 inches) in diameter. The spines can inflict a very painful wound. Courtesy of Ron Russo.

is said to be helpful in alleviating the pain. Immerse the wounded area in hot water (120°F or 50°C) for thirty to ninety minutes until pain is relieved, taking care not to scald the patient. If the spine is embedded, a local anesthetic will be required. Steroid creams and antibiotics may be needed. Contact dermatitis is best treated with the use of steroid creams and antihistamines.

Prevention: Care should be taken in handling this venomous starfish. If possible, wear heavy gloves. Only on the soft undersurface of the animal is it safe to make contact with bare hands.

Some sea urchins are of concern to skin divers because of their abundance and the ability of their sharp spines to penetrate sandals, shoes, and flippers. The long-spined tropical sea urchins (*Diadema* and its relatives) are especially hazardous. Persons diving in the West Indies should take special care because of the great abundance of these urchins in shallow water areas in many of the Caribbean Islands. Sea urchins are most commonly encountered under rocks, in crevices, or in other sheltered areas among corals. Sometimes they are found in open sandy flats.

Because of the large number of sea urchins, only a few of the more representative ones will be listed.

FAMILY DIADEMATIDAE

LONG-SPINED or BLACK SEA URCHIN, *Diadema setosum* (Leske) (fig. 3-49). Widely distributed throughout the Indo-Pacific area, from East Africa to Polynesia, China, and Japan. Closely related species are found in the West Indies and the Hawaiian Islands. The spines are dangerous.

FAMILY ECHINOTHURIDAE

SEA URCHIN, *Asthenosoma ijimai* Yoshiwara (fig. 3-50). Ranges from Southern Japan to the Molucca Sea. Possesses sharp venomous spines on the underside of the shell.

FAMILY TOXOPNEUSTIDAE

SEA URCHIN, *Toxopneustes elegans* Doderlein (fig. 3-51). Inhabits the waters about Japan. Possesses venomous pedicellariae.

SEA URCHIN, *Toxopneustes pileolus* (Lamarck) (fig. 3-52). Inhabits the Indo-Pacific area, from East Africa to Melanesia, and Japan. Possesses venomous pedicellariae.

Venom Apparatus of Sea Urchins: There are two types of venom organs in sea urchins: (1) venomous spines, and (2) their globiferous pedicellariae. Most of the dangerous species are equipped with either one or the other, but seldom both.

Fig. 3-49. **Long-spined Sea Urchin,** *Diadema setosum* (Leske). Spines may reach a length of 30.4 centimeters (12 inches) or more. Courtesy of D. Faulkner.

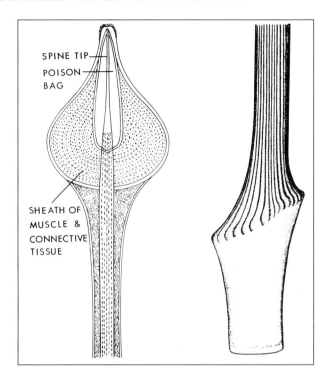

SPINE TIP
POISON
BAG

SHEATH OF
MUSCLE &
CONNECTIVE
TISSUE

Fig. 3-50. Spines of **Sea Urchin**, *Asthenosoma ijimai* Yoshiwara. Drawing by R. Kreuzinger after Mortensen.

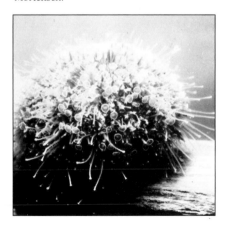

Fig. 3-51. **Sea Urchin**, *Toxopneustes elegans* Doderlein. Courtesy of T. Iwago. Diameter 7.5 centimeters (2.9 inches).

The spines of sea urchins vary greatly from group to group. In most instances the spines are solid, have blunt, rounded tips, and do not constitute a venom organ. However, some species have long, slender, hollow, sharp spines which are extremely dangerous to handle. The acute tips and the

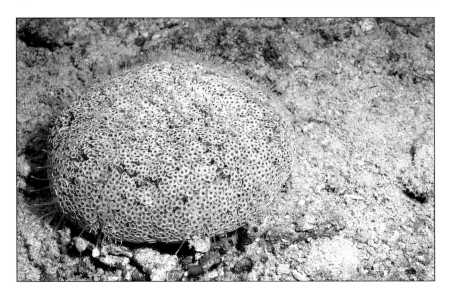

Fig. 3-52. **Venomous Sea Urchin,** *Toxopneustes pileolus* (Lamarck). The venomous globiferous pedicellariae appear as small flowerlike structures extending slightly beyond the spines. The pedicellariae of this species can inflict a painful sting, which may be lethal. Do not handle this species without heavy gloves. Taken from Komodo Island, Indonesia. Diameter 13 centimeters (5 inches). Courtesy of Ron and Valerie Taylor.

spinules permit ready entrance of the spines deep into the flesh, but because of their extreme brittleness the spinules break off readily in the wound and are very difficult to withdraw. The spines in *Diadema* may attain a length of a foot or more. It is believed that the spines of some of these species secrete a venom, but this has not been experimentally demonstrated. The aboral spines of *Asthenosoma* are developed into special venom organs carrying a single large gland. The point is sharp and serves as a means of introducing the venom.

Pedicellariae are small, delicate, seizing organs which are found scattered among the spines of the shell. There are several different types of pedicellariae. One of these, because of its globe-shaped head, is called the globiferous pedicellariae, and serves as a venom organ. The pedicellariae are composed of two parts, a terminal, swollen, conical head, which is armed with a set of calcareous pincerlike valves or jaws, and a supporting stalk (figs. 3-53 and 3-54). The head is attached to the stalk either directly by the muscles or by a long flexible neck. On the inner side of each valve is found a small elevation provided with fine sensory hairs. Contact with these sensory hairs causes the valves to close instantly. The outer surface

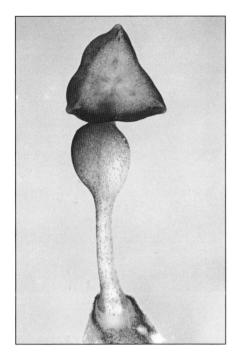

Fig. 3-53. The structure of the venomous pedicellarium with jaws open. The fang tips of the jaws can barely be seen at each point of the triangle protruding from the venom gland. Courtesy of P. Giacomelli.

Fig. 3-54. Globiferous pedicellariae from the **Sea Urchin**, *Salamacis bicolor* (Agassiz). This is representative of the venomous type of pedicellariae which are found in other species of sea urchins. Drawing by R. Kreuzinger after Mortensen.

of each valve is covered by a large gland, which in *Toxopneustes* has two ducts that empty in the vicinity of a small toothlike projection on the terminal fang of the valve. A sensory bristle is located on the inside of each valve. Contact with these bristles causes the small muscles at the base of the valve to contract, thus closing the valves and injecting the venom into the skin of the victim.

One of the primary functions of pedicellariae is that of defense. When the sea urchin is at rest in calm water, the valves are generally extended, moving slowly about, awaiting prey. When a foreign body comes in contact with them, it is immediately seized. The pedicellariae do not release their hold as long as the object moves, and if it is too strong to be held, the pedicellariae are torn from the test, or shell, but continue to bite the object. Detached pedicellariae may remain alive for several hours after being removed from the sea urchin, and may continue to secrete venom into the victim.

Medical Aspects: Penetration of the needle-sharp sea urchin spines may produce an immediate and intense burning sensation. The pain is soon followed by redness, swelling, and an aching sensation. Numbness and muscular paralysis have been reported and secondary infections are not uncommon.

The sting from sea urchin pedicellariae may produce an immediate, intense, radiating pain, faintness, numbness, generalized muscular paralysis, loss of speech, respiratory distress and, in severe cases, death. The pain may diminish after about fifteen minutes and completely disappear within an hour, but paralysis may continue for six hours or longer.

Treatment: The treatment of sea urchin wounds caused by their spines varies with the type of spine and the area of the body involved. Most sea urchin spines are friable and break off quite easily when grasped with a pair of forceps. Generally, it is difficult to remove sea urchin spines without surgical intervention. If the spine is situated in soft tissue away from the bone, it sometimes can be crushed by pummeling the area with the fist. Local anesthesia may be required for pain. This tends to fragment the spine and usually the pieces will be absorbed in a few days and disappear. In other cases, the spines may become encrusted and remain for many months, sometimes migrating to another site where they may have to be surgically removed. Sea urchin spines penetrating a bone joint should be X-rayed and surgically removed. Failure to remove them may result in a severe chronic inflammatory reaction. Surgical debridement and careful cleansing of the wound in order to remove all of the spine fragments will be needed. If there is pain or instability in the joint, splinting may be necessary. Since sea urchin wounds frequently become infected, hot soaks and antibiotic therapy may be required. Poultices may be useful.

Pedicellariae envenomations may produce severe reactions because they are more potent than the venom found in the spines of sea urchins. Any pedicellariae clinging to the skin should be promptly removed. Bathing the wound with alcohol or some other antiseptic solution is usually helpful. The affected part should be immersed in hot water (120°F or 50°C), being careful not to scald the patient. Artificial respiration may be required. Any allergic reactions can usually be controlled with the use of adrenalin and antihistaminics. Antibiotics may be required. There are no specific antivenins available for sea urchin stings.

Prevention: No sea urchin having elongated, needlelike spines should be handled. Moreover, leather and canvas gloves, shoes, and flippers do not afford protection. Care should be taken in handling any tropical species of short-spined sea urchin without gloves because of the pedicellariae. Because of the danger of coming in contact with sea urchins, a diver working at night in coral areas must exercise extreme care.

BRYOZOANS, OR MOSS ANIMALS—ECTOPROCTA

The bryozoans or moss animals are members of the phylum Ectoprocta. They are small animals that are found in both marine and freshwater. They are mainly colony builders and seldom more than 6 millimeters (.23 inches) in height. Bryozoan colonies are found encrusting on a variety of surfaces, including shells, rocks, large brown algae, mangrove roots, ship bottoms, and on the bottom of the sea.

Each member of a colony, the zoarium, lives in a tiny chamber called a zoecium, which is secreted by the organism's epidermis (fig. 3-55). The individual animal is called a zooid or feeding polyp and is composed of the lophophore, digestive tract, muscles, and nerve centers. The cystid is the body wall of the animal, together with its secreted exoskeleton. The exoskeleton or zoecium may consist of a gelatinous, or chitinous material, or it may be impregnated with small granules of sand depending upon the species. The general shape of the animal may be vaselike, boxlike, oval, or tubular, according to the species. The colonies vary in size and arrangement. At least one species has been incriminated as injurious to man. Bryozoans resemble seaweeds or hydroids. They differ from hydroids in that their tentacles are ciliated.

Fig. 3-55. Cluster of colonies (zoaria) of the bryozoan *Alcyonidium gelatinosum* (Linnaeus). Clusters vary in size from about 10.1 centimeters (4 inches) or more. Insert shows a single zoid in its case, termed the zoecium. Drawing by R.H. Knabenbauer.

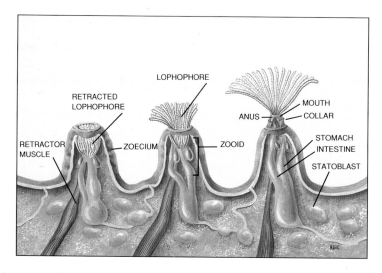

Fig. 3-56. A single colony (zoarium) of the bryozoan *A. gelatinosum* enlarged to show body parts. Stinging is caused by coming in contact with the lophophore. Drawing by R. H. Knabenbauer.

Fig. 3-57. "Dogger's Bank Itch," caused by contact with the bryozoan *Alcyonidium gelatinosum* (Linnaeus). J. Jeanmougin, courtesy of R. Mandojana.

FAMILY ALCYONIDIIDAE

Alcyonidium gelatinosum (Linnaeus) (fig. 3-56) is free growing, yellowish, yellow-brown, or grayish in color, and softly gelatinous, branched or cylindrical, and branched in structure. The colonies (zoaria) vary in size and arrangement depending upon the structure on which they are encrusted. The zoaria are about 6 millimeters in height. They may be fixed by a base attached to the sea bottom or some other object. *A. gelatinosum* ranges throughout the Arctic boreal and is circumpolar, found in both the Pacific and Atlantic oceans.

Medical Aspects: Contacts with this organism are generally made by fishermen removing fish with their bare hands from their drag nets and encountering colonies of these bryozoans. Skin contacts with these bryozoans may cause an irritating contact erythematous dermatitis, which is found primarily on the palms of the hands and forearms. This type of dermatitis occurs in the North Sea, where it is commonly referred to as Dogger's Bank itch (fig. 3-57).

Treatment: The use of topical steroid and antihistamine creams is helpful.

Prevention: Wear protective gloves and clothing to avoid contacts with stinging bryozoans.

CHAPTER 4

MARINE ANIMALS THAT STING: VERTEBRATES

Venomous marine vertebrates constitute a hazard to skin divers which, for the most part, can be easily avoided if the diver is aware of them and knows something about their habits. Included in this chapter are those marine animals having a backbone. These vertebrates inflict injury by stinging. Venomous marine vertebrates fall within two major groups: (1) fishes and (2) reptiles. A remarkable and interesting variety of venomous fishes is found to exist, beginning with some of the lower forms and extending throughout the piscine group. Venomous marine reptiles, on the other hand, are limited to a relatively few species—the sea snakes, all of which have a similar type of venom apparatus.

FISHES: HORNED OR SPINY SHARKS
FAMILY SQUALIDAE

There are several species of horned sharks, but only one that has been incriminated to any extent as producing stings in humans: The spiny dog-fish, *Squalus acanthias* Linnaeus (fig. 4-1), which is found on both sides of the North Atlantic and North Pacific Oceans. Some of its close relatives are widely distributed throughout temperate and tropical seas. Dogfish are somewhat sluggish in their movements, and seem to prefer shallow, pro-tected bays for their habitat.

Venom Apparatus: Wounds of the spiny dogfish are inflicted by the dorsal sting, which is located adjacent to the anterior margin of each of the two dorsal fins. The venom gland appears as a glistening, whitish substance situated in a shallow groove on the back of the upper portion of each spine. When the spine enters the skin, the venom gland is damaged, and the venom enters the flesh of the victim.

104

Fig. 4-1. **Spiny Dogfish,** *Squalus acanthias* Linnaeus. Note the single spine in front of each of the dorsal fins. Painting by R.H. Knabenbauer.

Medical Aspects: Symptoms consist of immediate, intense, stabbing pain, which may continue for a period of hours. The pain may be accompanied and followed by redness and severe swelling of the affected part, resulting in cellulitis. Tenderness about the wound may continue for several days. According to some authors, dogfish stings have been known to be fatal, which is probably due to bacterial contamination.

Treatment: See section on treatment of venomous fish stings, pages 158-60.

Prevention: Stings usually occur from the careless handling of dogfish. Be careful of the dorsal stings when removing the dogfish from a spear, hook, or net. Dogfish can give a sudden jerk and drive the sting deep into the flesh of a reckless fisherman.

STINGRAYS

Stingrays constitute one of the largest and most important groups of venomous marine organisms. There are said to be about 1,500 stingray attacks reported in the United States each year. Stingrays are divided into seven families:

1. Dasyatidae—stingrays or whiprays
2. Gymnuridae—butterfly rays
3. Mobulidae—devil rays or mantas

4. Myliobatidae—eagle rays or bat rays
5. Potamotrygonidae—river rays
6. Rhinopteridae—cownose rays
7. Urolophidae—round stingrays

The species within these families are too numerous to list individually, so only a few representative species, which have been studied to a considerable extent by venomologists, will be included. However, there are a few generalities which are pertinent to the group as a whole.

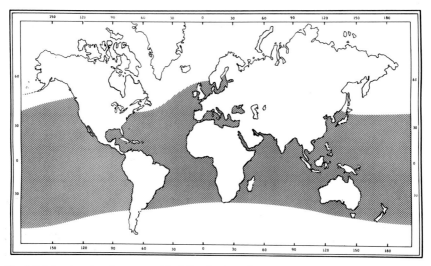

Fig. 4-2. Map showing the geographical distribution of stingrays.

Rays are common inhabitants of tropical, subtropical, and warm temperate seas (fig. 4-2). With the exception of the family Potamotrygonidae, which is confined to freshwater, rays are essentially marine forms, some of which may enter brackish, or freshwaters, freely. Although most common in shallow water, rays swim in moderate depths as well. A deep sea species has been reported from the Central Pacific Ocean. Sheltered bays, shoal lagoons, river mouths, muddy and sandy areas between patch reefs are favorite habitats of rays. They may be observed lying on top of the sand, or partially submerged, with only their eyes, spiracles, and a portion of the tail exposed. Rays burrow into the sand and mud, excavating with the use of their pectoral fins worms, molluscs, and crustaceans upon which they feed.

STINGRAYS OR WHIPRAYS, DASYATIDAE

GIANT STINGRAY OF AUSTRALIA, *Dasyatis brevicaudata* (Hutton). Inhabits the Indo-Pacific region (fig. 4-3). Reputed to be the largest stingray in the world, attaining a length of 4.5 meters (15 feet), a width of 2.1 meters (7 feet), and a weight of more than 325 kilograms (715 pounds).

DIAMOND STINGRAY, *Dasyatis dipterurus* (Jordan and Gilbert)(fig. 4-4). Occurs from British Columbia to Central America.

EUROPEAN STINGRAY, *Dasyatis pastinaca* (Linnaeus)(fig. 4-5). Inhabits the northeastern Atlantic Ocean, Mediterranean Sea, and Indian Ocean. It is a very common species.

BLUNTNOSE STINGRAY, *Dasyatis sayi* (Lesueur) (fig. 4-6). Inhabits the Western Atlantic from New Jersey to southern Brazil.

BUTTERFLY RAYS, GYMNURIDAE

BUTTERFLY RAY, *Gymnura marmorata* (Cooper) (fig. 4-7). Found from Point Conception, California, south to Mazatlán, Mexico.

DEVIL RAYS OR MANTAS, MOBULIDAE

DEVIL RAY, *Mobula mobular* (Bonnaterre). Found in the Atlantic Ocean. Not dangerous to man.

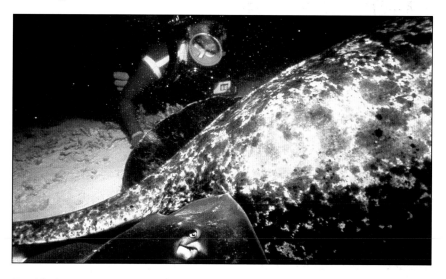

Fig. 4-3. **Giant Stingray**, *Dasyatis brevicaudata* (Hutton). Valerie Taylor swimming alongside this giant ray. Attains a length of 4.5 meters (15 feet) or more, and a width of 2.2 meters (7 feet). Reputed to be the largest stingray in the world. The head of a small shovel-nose ray is seen in the foreground. Great Barrier Reef, Australia. Courtesy of Ron and Valerie Taylor.

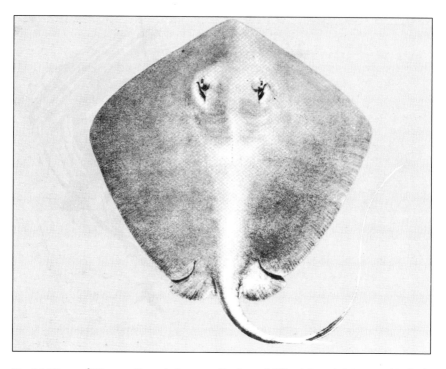

Fig. 4-4. **Diamond Stingray,** *Dasyatis dipterurus* (Jordan and Gilbert). Length 1.9 meters (6.5 feet). Drawing by M. Shirao.

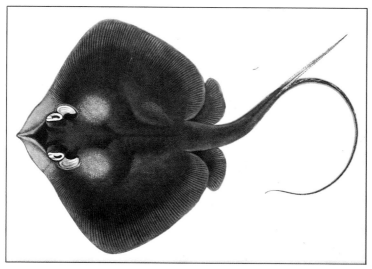

Fig. 4-5. **European Stingray,** *Dasyatis pastinaca* (Linnaeus). Length 2.4 meters (8 feet). Courtesy of Fish Resources of the U.S.S.R.

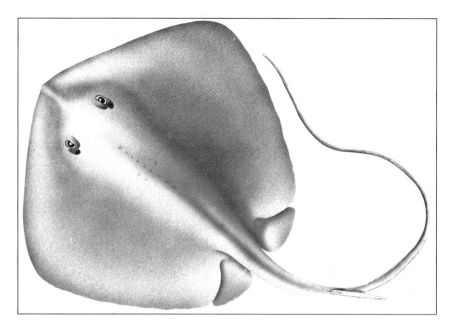

Fig. 4-6. **Bluntnose Stingray**, *Dasyatis sayi* (Lesueur). Length .9 meter (3 feet). Drawing by R. Kreuzinger.

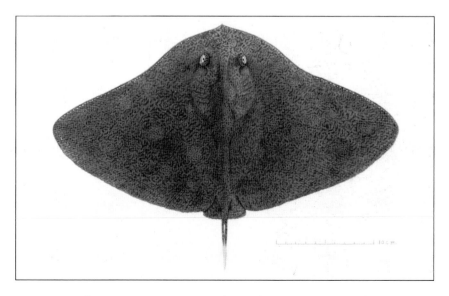

Fig. 4-7. **Butterfly Ray**, *Gymnura marmorata* (Cooper). Wingspan may reach 2.1 meters (7 feet). From Hiyama.

BAT RAYS OR EAGLE RAYS, MYLIOBATIDAE

SPOTTED EAGLE RAY, *Aetobatus narinari* (Euphrasen) (fig. 4-8). Inhabits tropical and warm-temperate belts of the Atlantic, Red Sea, and Indo-Pacific Oceans.

CALIFORNIA BAT RAY, *Myliobatis californicus* (Gill)(fig. 4-9). Found from Oregon to Magdalena Bay, Lower California.

FRESHWATER STINGRAYS, POTAMOTRYGONIDAE

SOUTH AMERICAN FRESHWATER STINGRAY, *Potamotrygon motoro* (Müller and Henle)(fig. 4-10). Found in the freshwater rivers of Paraguay, and the Amazon River, south to Rio de Janeiro, Brazil. It is an extremely dangerous species.

COWNOSE RAYS, RHINOPTERIDAE

COWNOSE RAY, *Rhinoptera bonasus* (Mitchill)(fig. 4-11). Found in the coastal western Atlantic, from New England to Brazil.

ROUND STINGRAYS, UROLOPHIDAE

ROUND STINGRAY, *Urolophus halleri* Cooper (fig. 4-12). Found from Point Conception, California, south to Panama Bay.

YELLOW STINGRAY, *Urolophus jamaicensis* (Cuvier) (fig. 4-13). Found in the western tropical Atlantic, from Florida southward into the Caribbean.

Venom Apparatus of Stingrays: The venom apparatus, or sting, of stingrays is an integral part of the caudal, or tail, appendage. A study of stingrays reveals that there are four general anatomical types of venom organs which vary somewhat in their effectiveness as a defensive weapon. The types are shown in figure 4-14.

1. *Gymnurid type.* This type is found in the butterfly rays (*Gymnura*). The sting is small, poorly developed, and situated close to the base of a short tail, making it a relatively feeble striking organ.

2. *Myliobatid type.* This type is found in the bat, or eagle rays (*Myliobatis, Aetobatis, Rhinoptera*). Their tails terminate in a long whiplike appendage. The stings in these rays are frequently large and well-developed, but situated near the base of the tail. Under the proper circumstances these rays can use their venom organs to good advantage.

3. *Dasyatid type.* This type is found in the stingrays proper (*Dasyatis*). The sting is well-developed as in the previous type, but is located further out from the base of the tail, making it a more effective striking organ. Stingrays

Fig. 4-8. **Bat Ray** or **Spotted Eagle Ray**, *Aetobatus narinari* (Euphrasen). This is one of the most handsome of the stingrays. The wingspan is about 2 meters (6.7 feet). Courtesy of R. Murphy, The Cousteau Society, Inc.

Fig. 4-9. **California Bat Ray**, *Myliobatis californicus* (Gill). This ray is frequently seen resting in sandy areas in the midst of a kelp forest or swimming in a gliding motion near the bottom. Taken at San Clemente Island. Length 1.2 meters (3.9 feet). Courtesy of California Fish and Game.

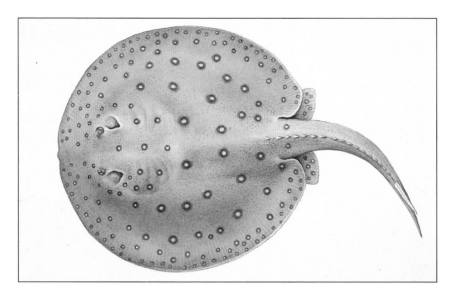

Fig. 4-10. **South American Freshwater Stingray**, *Potamotrygon motoro* (Müller and Henle).The width of the disc is 53.3 centimeters (21 inches). Courtesy of M. Shirao.

Fig. 4-11. **Cownose Rays,** *Rhinoptera bonasus* (Mitchill). Attains a width of about 1.9 meters (6.5 feet). Courtesy of J. Stebenaler.

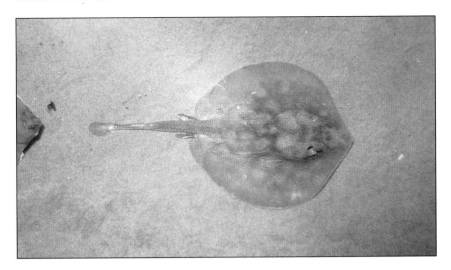

Fig. 4-12. A. **Round Stingray**, *Urolophus halleri* Cooper. Taken in southern California. Length 50 centimeters (19.7 inches). Courtesy of D. W. Gotshall.

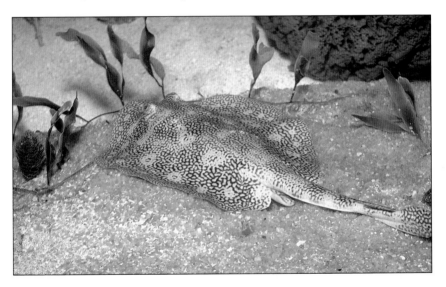

Fig. 4-13. **Yellow Stingray**, *Urolophus jamaicensis* (Cuvier). Length 67 centimeters (2.2 feet). Taken in Florida. Courtesy of R. Straughan.

possessing this type of venom apparatus are among the most dangerous kinds known. Their tails terminate in a long whiplike appendage.

4. *Urolophid type.* This type is found among the round stingrays (*Urolophus* and *Potamotrygon*). The caudal appendage to which the sting is attached

is short, muscular, and well-developed (fig. 4-15). Urolophid rays are also dangerous to man and can inflict a well-directed sting. In general, the venom apparatus of stingrays consists of the serrate spine and an enveloping sheath of skin. Together they are termed the sting. Stingrays usually possess only a single spine at a time, but it is not unusual to find a specimen with two or more. Apparently, the spine remains until it is removed by injury. There is no evidence to support the idea that the spines are shed each year. As the young spine grows out from the tail, it takes with it a layer of skin, the so-called integumentary sheath, which continues to ensheathe the spine until it is removed by injury or wear.

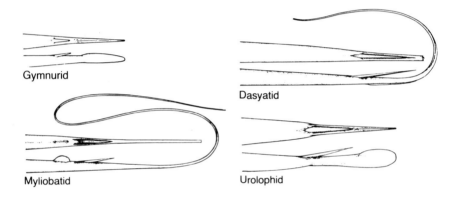

Fig. 4-14. Anatomical types of venom organs that are found in the various species of stingrays. (From Halstead and Bunker).

Fig. 4-15. Caudal appendage of *Myliobatis californicus*, the **California Bat Ray**. Note the tip of the sting protruding through the integumentary sheath. The venom glands are within the integumentary sheath. W.L.R.I. photo.

The spine is composed of a hard, bonelike material, called vasodentine. Along both sides of the spine are a series of sharp recurved teeth. The spine is marked by a number of irregular, shallow furrows which run almost the length of the spine. Along either edge, on the underside of the spine, there will be found deep grooves; these grooves are technically termed the ventro-lateral-glandular grooves. If these grooves are carefully examined, it will be observed that they contain a strip of soft, spongy, grayish tissue extending throughout their length. The bulk of the venom is produced by other portions of the integumentary sheath and in certain specialized areas of the skin on the tail adjacent to the spine. These grooves serve to protect the soft delicate glandular tissue which lies within them, and even though all of the integumentary sheath may be worn away, the venom-producing tissue continues to remain within these grooves. Thus, a perfectly clean-looking spine can still be venomous. Figure 4-16 illustrates the stingray sting in cross section. Figure 4-17 shows the caudal stings of various species of stingrays.

Medical Aspects: Pain is the predominant symptom and usually develops immediately or within a period of ten minutes following the attack. The

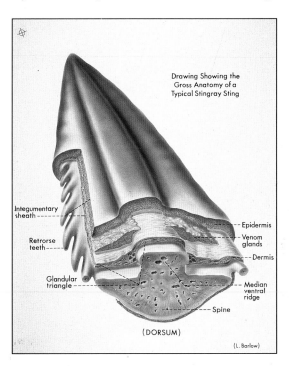

Fig. 4-16. Drawing showing the gross anatomy of a typical stingray sting. Drawing by L. Barlow.

Fig. 4-17. Caudal stings from various species of stingrays. A. *Myliobatis californicus*. B. *Aetobatus narinari*. C. *Dasyatis dipterurus*. D. *Urolophus halleri*. E. *Gymnura marmorata*. Dorsal and ventral views. All are spines except for *Gymnura marmorata*. Photo by R. Kreuzinger.

pain has been variously described as sharp, shooting, spasmodic, or throbbing in character. Freshwater stingrays are reputed to cause extremely painful wounds. More generalized symptoms of fall in blood pressure, vomiting, diarrhea, sweating, rapid heartbeat, muscular paralysis, and death have also been reported.

Stingray wounds are either of the laceration or puncture type (figs. 4-18, 4-19). Penetration of the skin and underlying tissue is usually accomplished without serious damage to the surrounding structures, but withdrawal of the sting may result in extensive tissue damage due to the recurved spines. Swelling in the vicinity of the wound is a constant finding. The area about the wound at first has an ashy appearance, later becomes cyanotic, and then reddens. Although stingray injuries occur most frequently about the ankle joint and foot as a result of stepping on the ray, instances have been reported in which the wounds were in the chest. Chest wounds may result in death.

Fig. 4-18. Heel injury caused by a boy stepping on a dead stingray. Courtesy of Robert D. Hayes.

Fig. 4-19. Stingray injury on right foot from an unidentified stingray species. Courtesy of R.C. Schoening.

Fig. 4-20. Drawing showing how stingray wounds are most frequently encountered. Drawing by R. Kreuzinger.

Treatment: There is no known specific antidote. See treatment of fish stings on pages 158-60.

Prevention: It should be kept in mind that stingrays commonly lie almost completely buried in the upper layer of a sandy or muddy bottom. They are, therefore, a hazard to anyone wading in water inhabited by them. The chief danger is in stepping on one that is buried (fig. 4-20). Since the body of the stingray is usually pinned down by the weight of the victim, thereby permitting the beast to make a successful strike, pushing or shuffling one's feet along the bottom eliminates the danger and at the same time chases the stingray from its lair. It is also recommended that a stick be used to probe along the bottom in order to rid the area of hidden rays.

ELEPHANTFISH AND RATFISH

Chimaeroids, elephantfish, or ratfish, as they are variously called, are a group of cartilaginous fishes having a single external gill opening on either side, covered over by a skin fold which leads to the gill chamber. Externally, rat-fishes are more or less compressed laterally, tapering posteriorly to a slender tail. The snout is rounded, or cone-shaped, extended as a long pointed beak, or bears a curious hoe-shaped proboscis. There are two dorsal fins. The first fin is triangular, usually higher than the second, and edged anteriorly by a strong, sharp-pointed bony spine which serves as a venom organ (fig. 4-21). Ratfishes have a preference for cooler waters, and have a depth range from the surface down to 1,400 fathoms (2,625 meters). They are weak swimmers and die soon after being removed from the water. They have well-developed dental plates and can inflict a nasty bite. Only two species have been studied to any extent by venomologists.

FAMILY CHIMAERIDAE

EUROPEAN RATFISH, *Chimaera monstrosa* Linnaeus (fig. 4-22). Inhabits the north Atlantic Ocean from Norway and Iceland to Cuba, the Azores, Morocco, the Mediterranean Sea, and South Africa.

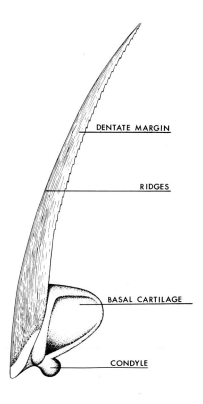

Fig. 4-21. Dorsal spine of the **Pacific ratfish**, *Hydrolagus colliei* (Lay and Bennett). From Halstead and Bunker.

Fig. 4-22. **European Ratfish**, *Chimaera monstrosa* Linnaeus. Length 1 meter (39 inches). Drawing by M. Shirao.

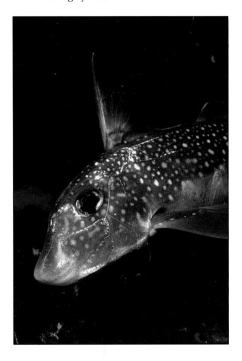

Fig. 4-23. **Pacific Ratfish**, *Hydrolagus colliei*. (Lay and Bennett). Length 1 meter (39 inches). Courtesy of Tom Stack.

PACIFIC RATFISH, *Hydrolagus colliei* (Lay and Bennett) (fig. 4-23). Found along the Pacific coast of North America.

Venom Apparatus of the Ratfish: The venom apparatus of ratfishes consists of the single dorsal sting which is situated along the anterior margin of the first dorsal fin. Along the back of the spine is a shallow depression which contains a strip of soft, grayish tissue—the venom gland.

Medical Aspects: Ratfishes inflict a very painful single puncture wound with their sharp dorsal stings. The pain is immediate and tends to increase in severity for a few minutes, and may continue to be severe for several hours, gradually lessening in intensity. A dull ache may continue for many days. The area about the wound may become numb to the touch and develop a cyanotic or blackish appearance. The outer area may be pale, swollen, and similar in appearance to a severe inflammatory reaction. Joint aches and swollen lymph nodes may be present. It is assumed that wounds from this fish are largely accidental, since the fish is not reputed to be aggressive. However, they are also equipped with powerful jaws and are capable of inflicting nasty bites. The viscera of these fish have been found to be toxic to laboratory animals.

CATFISHES

Catfishes come in a wide variety of sizes and body shapes, varying from short to greatly elongated, or even eellike. The head is sometimes very large, wide or depressed, or may be very small. The lips are usually equipped with long barbels. The skins of these fishes are thick and slimy, or may be covered with bony plates. No true scales are ever present. Included within this group are about one thousand species, most of which are found in the freshwater streams of the tropics. A few are marine. Only a few representative catfish species are listed.

FAMILY ARIIDAE

CATFISH, *Galeichthys felis* (Linnaeus) (fig. 4-24). Ranges from Cape Cod to the Gulf of Mexico.

Fig. 4-24. **Catfish,** *Galeichthys felis* (Linnaeus). This marine catfish is more active than most of its freshwater relatives. The pectoral and dorsal spines are very sharp and can inflict painful wounds. Length 39.8 centimeters (15.7 inches). Courtesy of Miami Seaquarium.

Fig. 4-25. **Sea Catfish**, *Bagre marinus* (Mitchill). This catfish has sharp spines that can inflict a very painful sting. Length 35 centimeters (13.7 inches). Courtesy of Miami Seaquarium.

Fig. 4-26. **Catfish**, *Clarias batrachus* (Linnaeus). Length 29.7 centimeters (11.7 inches). India to the Malay Archipelago and Philippine Islands. From Day.

FAMILY BAGRIDAE

SEA CATFISH, *Bagre marinus* (Mitchill) (fig. 4-25). Inhabits the east coast of America from Cape Cod to Rio de Janeiro, Brazil.

FAMILY CLARIIDAE

CATFISH, *Clarias batrachus* (Linnaeus) (fig. 4-26). India to the Malay Archipelago and Philippine Islands.

FAMILY HETEROPNEUSTIDAE

CATFISH, *Heteropneustes fossilis* (Bloch) (fig. 4-27). Found along the coasts of India, Sri Lanka, and Vietnam.

FAMILY PLOTOSIDAE

ORIENTAL CATFISH, *Plotosus lineatus* (Thunberg) (fig. 4-28). Occurs in the vicinity of river mouths throughout much of the Indo-Pacific area.

Fig. 4-27. **Catfish**, *Heteropneustes fossilis* (Bloch). Length 24.6 centimeters (9.7 inches). Found along the coasts of India, Sri Lanka, and Vietnam. From Day.

Fig. 4-28. **Oriental Catfish**, *Plotosus lineatus* (Thunberg). This catfish can inflict a very painful sting. Taken in Kuwait. Length 29.7 centimeters (11.7 inches). Courtesy of R.S. Criddle.

Venom Apparatus of Catfishes: Venomous catfishes have a single sharp, stout spine immediately in front of the soft-rayed portion of the dorsal and pectoral fins (fig. 4-29). This spine is enveloped by a thin layer of skin, the integumentary sheath, which is continuous with that of the soft-rayed portion of the fin. There is no external evidence of the venom glands, which are located as a series of glandular cells within the outer, or epidermal, layer of the integumentary sheath. The venom, or glandular, cells are most concentrated at the anterolateral and posterolateral margins of the sting where they are sometimes clumped two or three cells deep within the epidermal layer. The spines of some species are also equipped with a series of sharp, recurved teeth, which are capable of producing a severe laceration of the victim's flesh, thus facilitating absorption of the venom and subsequent secon-

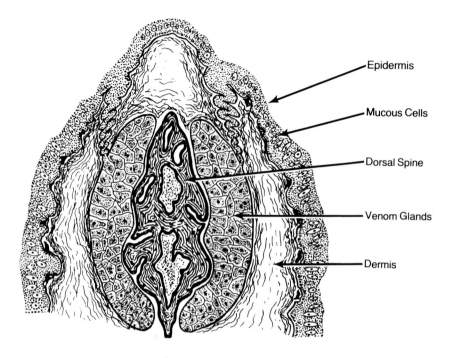

Epidermis

Mucous Cells

Dorsal Spine

Venom Glands

Dermis

Fig. 4-29. Drawing of a cross section of the dorsal sting of *Plotosus lineatus* (Thunberg). Note the large platelike arrangement of the venom glands, which cover most of the lateral surfaces of the dorsal spine. Drawing by R. Kreuzinger.

dary infection (fig. 4-30). The spines of the catfish are particularly dangerous because they can be locked into the extended position at the will of the fish.

Medical Aspects: The pain is generally described as an instantaneous stinging, throbbing, or scalding sensation which may be localized or may radiate up the affected limb. Some of the tropical species, such as *Plotosus*, are capable of producing violent pain which may last for forty-eight hours or more. Immediately after being stung, the area about the wound becomes pale. The pallor is soon followed by a cyanotic appearance, and then by redness and swelling. In some cases swelling may be very severe, accompanied by numbness and gangrene of the area about the wound. Shock may be present. Improperly treated cases frequently result in secondary bacterial infections of the wound. Because of recurved teeth along the margin of their spines, some species of catfishes may produce wounds which may take weeks to heal. Deaths have been reported from stings of some tropical catfishes.

Fig. 4-30. Fin spines of the **Catfish**, *Galeichthys felis* (Linnaeus). 1. Dorsal spine, posterior and side views. 2. Pectoral spine, dorsal and posterior views. Drawings by R. Kreuzinger.

Treatment: There are no known specific antidotes. See sections on treatment of fish stings on pages 158-60.

Prevention: Care should be exercised in the handling of catfishes because of their sharp rigid fin spines, which can be readily driven into the flesh of the unwary victim (fig. 4-31).

MORAY EELS
FAMILY MURAENIDAE

The bodies of these fishes are scaleless, elongated, and rounded, or more or less compressed. The dorsal and anal fins are continuous with the caudal, and are generally covered by thick skin. The pectoral and pelvic fins are absent.

The meager amount of research that has been conducted on so-called "venomous eels" is concerned with the single European species, *Muraena helena* Linnaeus (fig. 4-32), which is distributed along coastal areas of the eastern Atlantic Ocean and Mediterranean Sea. Other species have been

Fig. 4-31. Drawing showing how some catfishes are able to inflict a wound with their dorsal spine. Drawing by L.C. Innes.

listed as venomous by modern authors, but their opinions concerning these species are purely presumptive.

The teeth of *Muraena helena* have been considered as constituting a venom apparatus from earliest times. Anatomical studies fail to show any evidence of venom glands. However, it has been suggested that the palatine mucosa may secrete a toxic substance. The bite of a moray can be very painful and may become infected.

Treatment: Treat in the same manner as other types of fish stings and wounds.

Fig. 4-32. **European Moray Eel**, *Muraena helena* Linnaeus. This species attains a length of 1.5 meters (5 feet). (From Cevigon).

Fig. 4-33. **Greater Weever**, *Trachinus draco* Linnaeus. Occurs from Norway, British Isles, southward to the Mediterranean Sea, and along the coast of North Africa. Note that the fish is at rest with the dorsal fin depressed. The opercular spine is clearly evident on the gill cover. Length 44.9 centimeters (17.7 inches). Courtesy of P. Giacomelli.

WEEVERFISHES
FAMILY TRACHINIDAE

All weevers are small marine fishes which attain a maximum length of less than 45.7 centimeters (18 inches). They are among the more venomous fishes of the temperate zone. Primarily dwellers of flat, sandy, or muddy bays, weevers are commonly seen burying themselves in the soft sand or mud with only their heads partially exposed. They may dart out rapidly and may strike an object with their cheek spines with unerring accuracy. When a weever is provoked, the dorsal fin is instantly erected and the gill covers expanded. Because of their habit of concealment, aggressive attitude, and highly developed apparatus, they constitute a real danger to any skin diver working in their habitat. There are four species of weevers which are commonly recognized, but only two of them are included here.

GREATER WEEVER, *Trachinus draco* Linnaeus (fig. 4-33). Occurs from Norway, British Isles, southward to the Mediterranean Sea, and along the coast of North Africa.

LESSER WEEVER, *Trachinus vipera* Cuvier (fig. 4-34). Inhabits the North Sea, southward along the coast of Europe, and Mediterranean Sea.

Venom Apparatus of Weevers: The venom apparatus of the weeverfish consists of the dorsal and opercular spines and their associated glands (fig. 4-35). The dorsal spines vary from five to seven in number. Each of the spines is enclosed within a thin-walled sheath of skin from which protrudes a needle-sharp tip (fig. 4-36). Removal of the sheath reveals a thin, elongated, fusiform strip of whitish spongy tissue lying within the grooves, near the tips, of each spine. This spongy tissue is the venom-producing part of the spine. Removal of the skin covering the gill cover shows a broad, compressed, "daggerlike" opercular spine ending in a sharp tip. Attached to the upper and lower margins of the spine are the pear-shaped venom glands. Weever venom has been found to act as both a neurotoxin and hemotoxin, similar to some snake venoms.

Medical Aspects: Weever wounds usually produce instant pain, described as a burning, stabbing or "crushing" sensation—initially confined to the immediate area of the wound, then gradually spreading through the affected limb. The pain gets progressively worse until it reaches an excruciating peak, generally within thirty minutes. The severity is such that the victim may scream, thrash wildly about, and lose consciousness. In most instances, morphine fails to give relief. Untreated, the pain commonly

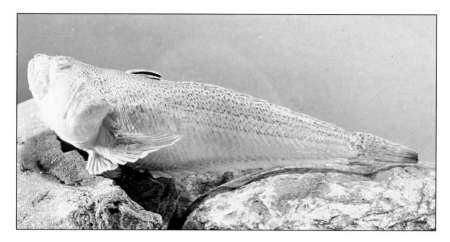

Fig. 4-34. **Lesser Weever**, *Trachinus vipera* Cuvier. Inhabits the North Sea, southward along the coast of Europe and Mediterranean Sea. The term "lesser" is in name only. Although this fish is smaller (15 centimeters [4.6 inches]) in size than the greater weeverfish, it can inflict an extremely painful sting. Courtesy of P. Giacomelli.

Fig. 4-35. Venom apparatus of *Trachinus draco* showing the venomous dorsal spines, inset, which are situated in lateral glandular grooves of the dorsal spine, and venom apparatus of the opercular spines, which are situated on the dorsal and ventral aspects of the opercular spines. The weeverfish is frequently buried in the sand and when aggravated can dart out of the sand and inflict an extremely painful wound using either the dorsal or opercular spines. Painting by R.H. Knabenbauer.

Fig. 4-37. Austrian diver stung by *Trachinus vipera* near Ischia Island, Naples, Italy. The diver was diving near a sandbank and came upon a lesser weever, which permitted the diver to touch it. Suddenly, the weever started moving in a snake-like fashion and quickly turned, facing the diver with fins vibrating in a most aggressive manner. Before the diver was able to withdraw, the weeverfish darted at him and struck him twice, first striking his mask and then his right jaw. The pain was intense and soon followed by respiratory distress. The right side of his face became severely swollen and cyanotic. The victim begged for someone to shoot him and put him out of his misery. The patient was taken to a hospital where he was given symptomatic treatment. Later he developed a massive hematoma on the right side of his face and neck as seen in this photograph. Gradually the patient's condition improved. The patient was discharged ten days after hospitalization. W.L.R.I. photo.

subsides within twenty-four hours. Tingling, followed by numbness, develops about the wound. The skin about the wound at first is blanched, but soon becomes reddened, hot, and swollen (fig. 4-37). The swelling may be quite extensive and continue for ten days or longer. Other symptoms consist of headache, fever, chills, delirium, nausea, vomiting, dizziness, sweating, cyanosis, joint aches, loss of speech, slow heartbeat, palpitation, mental depression, convulsions, difficulty in breathing, and death. Secondary infections are common in cases improperly treated. Gangrene has been known to develop as a complication. Recovery may take from several days to several months, depending upon the amount of venom received, condition of the patient, and other factors.

Treatment: There are no known antidotes. Same as the treatment of fish stings (see pages 158-60).

◄ Fig. 4-36. From top, head of *Trachinus*, showing the dorsal and opercular stings. Dorsal spine of *Trachinus vipera*, showing grooves in which the venom glands are located. Side and posterior views. Operculum of *Trachinus vipera* showing the daggerlike spine to which the venom gland is attached. Side view and cross section. Lateral view of left opercular sting of *Trachinus draco*. The integumentary sheath has been removed to show the venom glands which are seen as triangular masses lying above and below the shaft of the opercular spine. Drawing by R. Kreuzinger.

Prevention: Weeverfish stings are most commonly encountered while wading or swimming along sandy coastal areas of the eastern Atlantic or Mediterranean seas. Weevers are usually encountered partially buried in the sand or mud. Persons wading in waters where weevers abound should wear adequate footwear. Skin divers should avoid antagonizing these fishes since they are easily provoked into stinging. A living weever should never be handled under any circumstances. Even when dead, weevers can inflict a nasty wound.

SCORPIONFISHES
FAMILY SCORPAENIDAE

The scorpionfishes are widely distributed throughout all tropical and temperate seas. A few species are also found in arctic waters. Many Scorpaenidae attain large size and are valuable food fishes, whereas others are relatively small and of no commercial value. Some species are extremely venomous.

Venomous scorpionfishes have been divided into three main groups on the basis of the structure of their venom organs, namely: (1) Zebrafish (*Pterois*), (2) Scorpionfish proper (*Scorpaena*), and (3) the Stonefishes (*Synanceja*).

Zebrafish are among the most beautiful and ornate of coral reef fishes. They are generally found in shallow water, hovering about in a crevice or at times swimming unconcernedly in the open. They are also called turkeyfish because of their interesting habit of swimming around slowly and spreading their fanlike pectorals and lacy dorsal fins like a turkey gobbler displaying its plumes. These fish are frequently observed swimming in pairs, and are apparently fearless in their movements. Acceptance of an invitation to reach out and grab one of these fish results in an extremely painful experience, because hidden under the "lace" are needlesharp fin stings. The fearlessness of the zebrafish makes it a particular menace to anyone working in its habitat, the shallow water coral reef areas.

Members of the genus *Scorpaena* are for the most part shallow water, bottom-dwellers, found in bays, along sandy beaches, rocky coastlines, or coral reefs, from the intertidal zone to depths of 93 meters (50 fathoms) or more. Their habit of concealing themselves in crevices, among debris, under rocks, or in seaweed, together with their protective coloration, which blends them almost perfectly into their surrounding environment, makes them difficult to see. When they are removed from the water, they have the defensive habit of erecting their spinous dorsal fin and flaring out their armed gill covers, pectoral, pelvic, and anal fins. The pectoral fins, although dangerous in appearance, are unarmed.

Stonefishes are largely shallow-water dwellers, commonly found in tidepools and shoal reef areas. *Synanceja* has the habit of lying motionless in coral crevices, under rocks, in holes, or buried in sand and mud. They appear to be fearless and completely disinterested in the careless intruder.

ZEBRAFISH TYPE

ZEBRAFISH, LIONFISH, or TURKEYFISH, *Pterois volitans* (Linnaeus) (fig. 4-38). Inhabits the Red Sea, Indian Ocean, China, Japan, Australia, Melanesia, Micronesia, and Polynesia. One of several closely allied species found around coral reefs.

SCORPIONFISH TYPE

BULLROUT or SULKY, *Apistus carinatus* (Bloch and Schneider) (fig. 4-39). Inhabits the coast of India, the Malay Archipelago, Philippine Islands, China, Japan, and Australia.

WASPFISH or FORTESCUE, *Centropogon australis* (White)(fig. 4-40). Inhabits New South Wales and Queensland, Australia.

BULLROUT, *Notesthes robusta* (Günther)(fig. 4-41). Inhabits New South Wales and Queensland, Australia.

Fig. 4-38. **Zebrafish, Lionfish** or **Turkeyfish,** *Pterois volitans* (Linnaeus). Inhabits the Red Sea, Indian Ocean, China, Japan, Australia, Melanesia, Micronesia, and Polynesia. One of several closely allied species found around coral reefs. A very attractive and enticing fish but dangerous to touch since its fins are equipped with venom. Length 27.9 centimeters (11 inches). Courtesy of Paul Saunders.

Fig. 4-39. **Bullrout** or **Sulky**, *Apistus carinatus* (Bloch and Schneider). Dorsal and anal spines are venomous. Found in the Indo-Pacific and Indian Ocean. Length 15.71 centimeters (6.2 inches) or more. Painting by M. Shirao.

Fig. 4-40. **Waspfish** or **Fortescue**, *Centropogon australis* (White). Inhabits New South Wales and Queensland, Australia. This fish has been appropriately named the "Waspfish" because of the painful stings that it is capable of inflicting with its dorsal spines. Length 15.2 centimeters (6 inches). Courtesy of Justice F. Myers.

CALIFORNIA SCORPIONFISH, *Scorpaena guttata* Girard (fig. 4-42). Ranges from central California south into the Gulf of California.

SCORPIONFISH, *Scorpaena plumieri* Bloch (fig. 4-43). Inhabits the Atlantic coast from Massachusetts to the West Indies and Brazil. One of several closely related species found in this general region.

SCORPIONFISH, RASCASSE, SEA PIG, etc., *Scorpaena porcus* (Linnaeus) (fig. 4-44). Inhabits the Atlantic coast of Europe from the English Channel to the Canary Islands, French Morocco, Mediterranean and Black Seas.

DEVIL SCORPIONFISH, *Scorpaenopsis diabolus* (Cuvier)(fig. 4-45). Inhabits the Malay Archipelago, Australia, Melanesia, and Polynesia.

ROCKFISH, *Sebastes marinus* (Linnaeus) (fig. 4-46). Many of the rock-fish species found along the coastal areas of North America are now known to possess a venom apparatus and should be handled with care.

LUPO, *Inimicus japonicus* (Cuvier)(fig. 4-47). Inhabits the coastal areas of Japan.

STONEFISH TYPE

STONEFISH, *Choridactylus multibarbis* Richardson (fig. 4-48). Found along coastal areas of India, China, Philippine Islands, and Polynesia.

HIME-OKOZE, *Minous monodactylus* (Bloch and Schneider)(fig. 4-49). Inhabits the South Pacific islands, China, and Japan.

DEADLY STONEFISH, *Synanceja horrida* (Linnaeus); also *S. verrucosa* Bloch and Schneider (figs. 4-50, 4-51, and 4-52). Inhabits Indo-Pacific. Extremely dangerous species.

Venom Apparatus of Scorpionfishes: The venom organs of scorpion-fishes vary markedly from one group to the next. A comparison of some of the more important differences appears in the chart on page 143 (see also fig. 4-53).

The zebrafish, or *Pterois* type, has a venom apparatus consisting of thirteen dorsal spines, three anal spines, two pelvic spines, and their associated venom glands. The spines are for the most part long, straight, slender, and camouflaged in delicate, lacy-appearing fins. Located on the front side of each spine are the glandular grooves, open on either side, which appear as deep channels extending the entire length of the shaft. Situated within these grooves are the venom glands. The glands are enveloped in a thin covering of skin—the integumentary sheath.

The scorpionfish, or *Scorpaena* type, have a variable number of dorsal spines, frequently twelve, three anal, and two pelvic spines, and their

Fig. 4-41. **Bullrout,** *Notesthes robusta* (Günther). Inhabits New South Wales and Queensland, Australia. Length 24.6 centimeters (9.7 inches). Painting by S. Arita after Bleeker.

Fig. 4-42. **California Scorpionfish,** *Scorpaena guttata* Girard. Ranges from central California south into the Gulf of California. The color of this fish changes greatly depending upon the background upon which the fish is resting. The scorpionfish is adept at camouflage and may be difficult to detect, which in itself presents problems in attempting to avoid contact with venomous spines. Length 43.2 centimeters (17 inches). Courtesy of A. Giddings, Ocean Images, Inc.

Fig. 4-43. **Scorpionfish**, *Scorpaena plumieri* Bloch. Inhabits the Atlantic coast from Massachusetts to the West Indies and Brazil. One of several closely related species found in this general region. When the dorsal spines are erected, the fish is taking on an aggressive stance getting ready to strike its victim. Length 30.4 centimeters (12 inches). Courtesy of A. Bruce Bowker, Aquaventure Bonaire, N.A.

Fig. 4-44. **Scorpionfish, Rascasse, Sea Pig**, *Scorpaena porcus* (Linnaeus). Inhabits the Atlantic coast of Europe from the English Channel to the Canary Islands, French Morocco, Mediterranean and Black Seas. Fish is showing aggressive behavior. Length 30.4 centimeters (12 inches). From Fish Resources of the U.S.S.R.

Fig. 4-45. **Devil Scorpionfish**, *Scorpaenopsis diabolus* (Cuvier). Inhabits the Malay Archipelago, Australia, Melanesia, and Polynesia. A number of scorpionfishes, particularly of the genus *Scorpaenopsis*, closely resemble in appearance the deadly stonefish, *Synanceja*, and are confused with them. Both groups possess venom organs and are capable of inflicting painful stings. Length 25.4 centimeters (10 inches). Taken at Oahu, Hawaii. Courtesy of R.F. Myers.

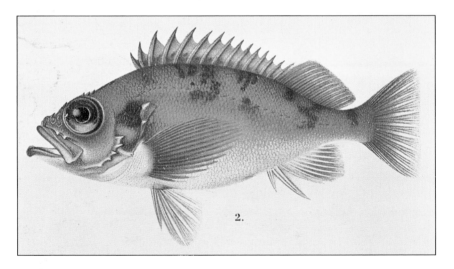

Fig. 4-46. **Rockfish**, *Sebastes marinus* (Linnaeus). Length 30.5 centimeters (12 inches). Many of the rockfish species found along the coastal areas of North America are now known to possess a venom apparatus and should be handled with care. From Smitt.

Fig. 4-47. **Lupo,** *Inimicus japonicus* (Cuvier). Length 20.3 centimeters (8 inches). Inhabits the coastal areas of Japan. Painting by M. Shirao.

Fig. 4-48. **Stonefish,** *Choridactylus multibarbus* Richardson. Length 10.2 centimeters (4 inches). Found along coastal areas of India, China, Philippine Islands, and Polynesia. Courtesy of J. Randall.

Fig. 4-49. **Hime-Okoze,** *Minous monodactylus* (Bloch and Schneider). Length 15.2 centimeters (6 inches). Inhabits the South Pacific islands, China, and Japan. From Bleeker.

Fig. 4-50. **Deadly Stonefish,** *Synanceja horrida* (Linnaeus). Length 60.9 centimeters (24 inches). Inhabits India, East Indies, China, Philippine Islands, and Australia. The stonefish is an extremely dangerous species. Drawing by M. Shirao.

Fig. 4-51. **Warty Deadly Stonefish**, *Synanceja verrucosa* Bloch and Schneider. Inhabits the Indo-Pacific. Resembles *S. horrida*, but lacks the deep depression behind the eyes. It is also similar in size. Length 30.4 centimeters (12 inches). Photo taken at Torres Strait, North Australia. Courtesy of K. Gillett.

associated venom glands. The spines are shorter and heavier than those found in *Pterois*. The glandular grooves are restricted to about the distal two-thirds of the spine. The venom glands lie along the glandular grooves, but are limited to about the distal half of the spine. The enveloping integumentary sheath is moderately thick.

The stonefish, or *Synanceja* type, usually have thirteen dorsal spines, three anal spines, two pelvic spines, and their associated venom glands. The venom organs of this fish differ from the others by the short, heavy spines and greatly enlarged venom glands which are covered by a very thick layer of warty skin. This fish is particularly dangerous because of its camouflaged appearance—frequently resembling a large clump of mud or debris. The stings of *Synanceja* are difficult to detect because they are almost completely hidden (fig. 4-54).

Medical Aspects: Symptoms produced by the various species of scorpionfishes are essentially the same, varying in degree, rather than in quality. The pain is usually described as immediate, intense, sharp, shooting, or throbbing, and radiates from the affected part. The area about the wound becomes ischemic, and then cyanotic. The pain produced by most scorpionfishes generally continues for only a few hours, but wounds produced by

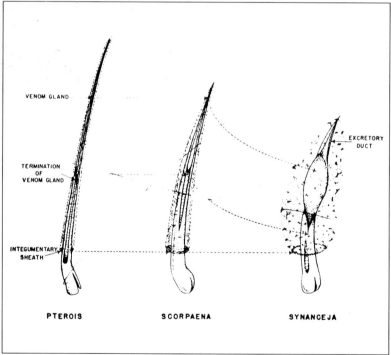

Fig. 4-53. A comparison of the three types of scorpionfish dorsal stings. Drawing by R. Kreuzinger.

◀ Fig. 4-52. **Deadly Stonefish,** *Synanceja horrida* (Linnaeus). This is not only one of the most repulsive looking of marine organisms, but also one of the most venomous. Stonefish are danger-ous to encounter because of their abil-ity to hide in the sand and their close resemblance to the coral habitat in which they conceal themselves. There are at least four different species, but only two of the more common ones are shown. *S. horrida* can be recognized by the deep indentation on the head immediately behind the eyes. Length 60.9 centimeters (24 inches). Photo taken at Heron Island, Great Barrier Reef, Australia. Courtesy of K. Gillett.

Fig. 4-54. Photograph of anterior view of first dorsal sting of the **Stonefish,** *Synanceja horrida* (Linnaeus). The in-tegumentary sheath has been peeled back to show the large venom glands situated on either side of the spine shaft. Length of spine 36 millimeters (1.3 inches). Photo by R. Kreuzinger.

Synanceja may be extremely painful and may continue for a number of days. Pain caused by *Synanceja* is sometimes so severe as to cause the victim to thrash about wildly, to scream, and, finally, to lose consciousness. The area in the immediate vicinity of the wound gradually becomes cyanotic sur-rounded by a zone of redness, swelling, and heat (figs. 4-55 and 4-56). Sub-sequent sloughing of the tissues about the wound site may occur. In the case

COMPARISON OF THE VENOM ORGANS

Structure	*Pterois*	*Scorpaena*	*Synanceja*
Fin spines	Elongated, slender	Moderately long, heavy	Short, stout
Integumentary sheath	Thin	Moderately thick	Very thick
Venom glands	Small-sized, well developed	Moderate-sized, very well-developed	Very large, highly developed
Venom duct	Not evident	Not evident	Well-developed

of *Synanceja* stings, the wound becomes numb, and the skin, some distance from the site of injury, becomes painful to touch. In some instances, complete paralysis of the limb may ensue. Swelling of the entire member that is affected may take place, frequently to such an extent that movement of the part is impaired. Other symptoms which may be present are: cardiac failure, delirium, convulsions, various nervous disturbances, nausea, vomiting, lymphangitis, swelling of the lymph nodes, joint aches, fever, respiratory distress, convulsions, and death. Complete recovery from a severe *Synanceja* sting may require many months, and may have an adverse effect on the general health of the victim.

Treatment: See section on treatment of venomous fish stings, pages 158-60.

Prevention: Zebrafish stings are usually contracted by individuals who are attracted by the slow movements and lacy-appearing fins and who attempt to pick the fish up with their hands. Most scorpionfish stings result when an individual removes the fish from the hook, or nets, and is jabbed by their venomous spines. Stonefish are especially dangerous because of the difficulty of detecting them from their surroundings. Placing one's hands in crevices, or in holes inhabited by these fishes, should be done with caution. Knowledge of the habits and appearance of these fishes is most important.

Fig. 4-55. Sting inflicted by the **Stonefish**, *Synanceja verrucosa* Bloch and Schneider, a closely related species to *Synanceja horrida*. The patient had been without treatment for three weeks and the finger had become gangrenous. Taken on Guam. Courtesy of R.C. Schoening.

Fig. 4-56. Stonefish sting on the left foot of a twenty-one-year-old female from Saipan. Identification of stonefish unknown. Courtesy of T. Rulison.

TOADFISHES
FAMILY BATRACHOIDIDAE

All toadfishes are small, bottom fishes which inhabit the warmer waters of the coasts of America, Europe, Africa, and India. With broad, depressed heads and large mouths, toadfishes are somewhat repulsive in appearance. Most of them are marine, but some are estuarine, or entirely freshwater, ascending rivers for great distances. They hide in crevices, burrows, under rocks, debris, among seaweed, or lie almost completely buried under a few centimeters of sand or mud. Toadfishes tend to migrate to deeper water during the winter months where they remain in a torpid state. They are experts at camouflage. Their ability to change to lighter or darker shades of color at will and their mottled pattern make these fishes difficult to see. Descriptions of some species follow.

TOADFISH, *Barchatus cirrhosus* (Klunzinger) (fig. 4-57). Inhabits the Red Sea.

TOADFISH, or MUNDA, *Batrachoides grunniens* (Linnaeus) (fig. 4-57). Inhabits the coasts of Sri Lanka, India, Myanmar, and Malaysia.

TOADFISH, *Batrachoides didactylus* (Bloch) (fig. 4-57). Inhabits the Mediterranean Sea and nearby Atlantic coasts.

TOADFISH, OYSTERFISH, *Opsanus tau* (Linnaeus) (fig. 4-58). Found along the Atlantic Coast of the United States, from Massachusetts to the West Indies.

TOADFISH, SAPO, *Thalassophryne maculosa* Günther (fig. 4-58). Inhabits the West Indies.

TOADFISH, BAGRE SAPO, SAPO, *Thalassophryne reticulata* Günther (fig. 4-58). Inhabits the Pacific Coast of Central America.

In addition to the above, there are several other closely related species inhabiting certain coastal areas of Central and South America.

Venom Apparatus: The venom apparatus of toadfishes consists of two dorsal fin spines, two gill cover spines, and their associated venom glands. The dorsal spines are slender and hollow, slightly curved, and terminate in sharp, needlelike points. At the base and tip of each spine is an opening through which the venom passes. The base of each dorsal spine is surrounded by a glandular mass from which the venom is produced. Each gland empties into the base of its respective spine (fig. 4-59). The operculum is also highly specialized as a defensive organ for the introduction of venom. The horizontal limb of the operculum is a slender, hollow bone which curves

Fig. 4-57. *Top,* **Toadfish,** *Barchatus cirrhosus* (Klunzinger). Length 25.4 centimeters (10 inches). *Middle,* **Toadfish,** *Batrachoides grunniens* (Linnaeus). Length 20.3 centimeters (8 inches). (From Sauvage). *Bottom, Batrachoides didactylus* (Bloch). Length 19 centimeters (7.5 inches). (From Steindachner).

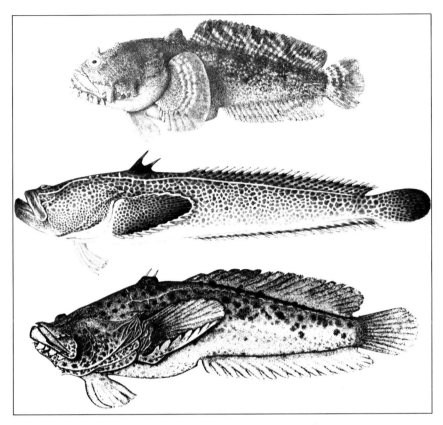

Fig. 4-58. *Top,* **Toadfish, Oysterfish,** *Opsanus tau* (Linnaeus). Length 29.7 centimeters (11.7 inches). *Middle,* **Toadfish,** *Thalassophryne reticulata* Günther. Length 25.4 centimeters (10 inches). *Bottom,* **Toadfish,** *Thalassophryne maculosa* Günther. Length 13.9 centimeters (5.5 inches). (From Collette).

slightly and terminates in a sharp tip. Openings are present at each end of the spine for the passage of venom. With the exception of the outer tip, the entire gill spine is encased within a glistening, whitish, pear-shaped mass. The broad, rounded portion of this mass is situated at the base of the spine, and tapers rapidly as the tip of the spine is approached. This mass is the venom gland. The gland empties into the base of the hollow gill spine, which serves as a duct.

Medical Aspects: The pain from toadfish wounds develops rapidly and is radiating and intense. Some have described the pain as being similar to that of a scorpion sting. The pain is soon followed by swelling, redness, and heat. No fatalities have been recorded in the literature, but little else is known about the effects of toadfish venom.

Fig. 4-59. Anatomy of the venom apparatus of the **Toadfish**, *Thalassophryne dowi*. A. Opercular sting. B. Dorsal sting. C. Photograph of the dorsal stings. The integumentary sheath has been removed to expose the large venom glands at the base of the two dorsal spines. Length of spines 11 millimeters (.4 inch). D. Left opercular sting. The skin has been removed to expose the venom gland. The opening of the venom canal is barely visible at the tip of the spine. Length of spine 10 millimeters (.3 inch). Drawings and photos by R. Kreuzinger.

Treatment: See section on treatment of venomous fish stings, pages 158-60.

Prevention: To avoid stepping on toadfish, persons wading in waters inhabited by them should take the precaution to shuffle their feet through the mud. Removal of toadfishes from a hook or from nets should be done with care.

SURGEONFISHES
FAMILY ACANTHURIDAE

Surgeonfishes are reef dwellers of warm seas. The principal genus of this family, *Acanthurus*, is characterized by the presence of a sharp, lancelike, movable spine on the side, at the base of the tail fin (fig. 4-60). When the fish becomes excited, the spine, the point of which is directed forward, can be extended at right angles from the body of the fish. With a quick, lashing movement of the tail and the extended spine, large surgeonfishes are likely to inflict a deep and painful wound. Under normal circumstances, the spine remains adducted within a deep recess partially surrounded by an integumentary sheath. It has not been fully determined whether the spines of surgeonfishes are venomous. Some species appear to have venomous spines whereas others do not. Therefore, all surgeonfishes should be handled with care.

Fig. 4-60. Tail of surgeonfish, showing the caudal spine in an extended position and ready to inflict a cut. Photo by D. Ollis.

Fig. 4-61. **Bleeker's Surgeonfish,** *Acanthurus bleekeri* Günther. Length 30 centimeters (11.8 inches). Found throughout the Indo-Pacific area, with the exception of Hawaii. From Hiyama.

SPECIES OF SURGEONFISHES

BLEEKER'S SURGEONFISH, *Acanthurus bleekeri* Günther (fig. 4-61). Found throughout the Indo-Pacific area, with the exception of Hawaii.

YELLOW-FINNED SURGEONFISH, *Acanthurus xanthopterus* Cuvier and Valenciennes (fig. 4-62.) Indo-Pacific area.

UNICORNFISH, *Naso lituratus* Bloch and Schneider (fig. 4-63). Ranges from Polynesia to east Africa and the Red Sea.

Medical Aspects: Surgeonfish wounds are usually of the laceration type. Larger specimens are capable of inflicting deep and painful wounds. Secondary infections may occur.

Treatment: See section on treatment of venomous fish stings, pages 158-60.

DRAGONETS
FAMILY CALLIONYMIDAE

Dragonets are small, scaleless fishes with flat heads, bearing a preopercle that is armed with a strong spine. These fishes are brightly variegated in color, and have high and often filamentous dorsal fins. Some species are

Fig. 4-62. **Yellow-Finned Surgeonfish**, *Acanthurus xanthopterus* Cuvier and Valenciennes. Indo-Pacific area. Length 35.6 centimeters (14 inches). Painting by G. Coates.

Fig. 4-63. **Unicornfish**, *Naso lituratus* Bloch and Schneider. This fish has fixed, nonmoveable forward-curved caudal spines at the base of the caudal fin, which can inflict a nasty cut. Length 38.1 centimeters (15 inches). Taken at Oahu, Hawaii. Courtesy of R. Russo.

Fig. 4-64. **Dragonet**, *Callionymus lyra* Linnaeus. *A*. Male. *B*. Female. Note preopercular spines, which are believed to be venomous. From Poll.

found in deep water, whereas others are shore fishes inhabiting shallow bays and reefs. The gill spine of the European species, *Callionymus lyra* Linnaeus (fig. 4-64), which is distributed along the Atlantic coast of Europe and the Mediterranean Sea, is said to be venomous. Dragonets are also considered to be capable of inflicting serious wounds. They should be handled with care.

RABBITFISHES
FAMILY SIGANIDAE

Rabbitfishes are a group of spiny-rayed fishes which closely resemble surgeonfishes. They differ from all other fishes in that the first and last rays of the pelvic fins are spinous. Usually valued as food, rabbitfishes are of moderate size, and abound about rocks and reefs from the Red Sea to Polynesia.

SPECIES OF RABBITFISHES

RABBITFISH, *Siganus fuscescens* (Houttuyn)(fig. 4-65). Found throughout the Indo-Pacific region.

RABBITFISH, *Siganus lineatus* (Valenciennes)(fig. 4-66). Inhabits the Philippines, Santa Cruz Islands, New Guinea, Solomon Islands, Australia, Okinawa, and the Ryukyu Islands.

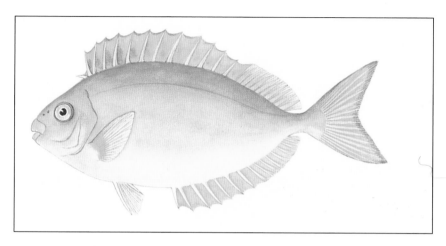

Fig. 4-65. **Rabbitfish**, *Siganus fuscescens* (Houttuyn). Length 24.6 centimeters (9.7 inches). Found throughout the Indo-Pacific region. From Hiyama.

RABBITFISH, *Siganus puellus* (Schlegel)(fig. 4-67). Inhabits the East Indies, Philippines, Palau, Gilbert, Marshall, and Solomon Islands.

Venom Apparatus: The venom apparatus of *Siganus* consists of thirteen dorsal, four pelvic, and seven anal spines, and their associated venom glands. A groove extends along both sides of the midline of the spine for almost its entire length. These grooves are generally deep and contain the venom glands, which are located in the outer one-third of the spine, near the tip (fig. 4-68).

Medical Aspects: The symptoms produced by rabbitfish stings are said to be similar to those produced by scorpionfishes. There is no information available regarding the nature of the venom.

Treatment: Same as treatment of venomous fish stings, pages 158-60.

Prevention: In handling rabbitfishes, one should be careful to avoid being jabbed with the dorsal, pelvic, or anal stings.

STARGAZERS
FAMILY URANOSCOPIDAE

Stargazers are bottom-dwelling marine fishes, members of the family Uranoscopidae, having a cuboid head, an almost vertical mouth with fringed lips, and eyes on the flat upper surface of the head. Uranoscopids spend a large part of their time buried in the mud or sand, with only their eyes and a portion of the mouth protruding.

Fig. 4-66. **Rabbitfish**, *Siganus lineatus* (Valenciennes). Length 29.7 centimeters (11.7 inches). Inhabits the Philippines, Santa Cruz Islands, New Guinea, Solomon Islands, Australia, Okinawa, and the Ryukyu Islands. Painting by G. Coates.

Fig. 4-67. **Rabbitfish**, *Siganus puellus* (Schlegel). Inhabits the East Indies, Philippines, Palau, Gilbert, Marshall, and Solomon Islands. Length 26.6 centimeters (10.5 inches). Taken at Palau. Courtesy of R.F. Myers.

Fig. 4-68. Venom apparatus of the **Rabbitfish**, *Siganus fuscescens.* Tip of the fifth dorsal sting of *Siganus fuscescens.* The skin has been removed to expose the venom gland (see arrow). The venom gland appears as a strip of tissue lying within the groove of the spine. Length of spine is 15 millimeters (.58 inch). Photo by R. Kreuzinger.

SPECIES OF STARGAZERS

STARGAZER or MISHMIMAOKOZE, *Uranoscopus japonicus* Houttuyn (fig. 4-69). Inhabits southern Japan, southern Korea, China, Philippine Islands, and Singapore.

STARGAZER, *Uranoscopus scaber* (Linnaeus) (fig. 4-70). Inhabits the eastern Atlantic and Mediterranean Sea.

Venom Apparatus: The venom apparatus of *Uranoscopus* is said to consist of two shoulder spines, one on either side, each of which protrudes through a sheath of skin (fig. 4-71). Venom glands are attached to these spines. The spine is said to have a double groove through which the venom flows.

Medical Aspects: There is no information available regarding the clinical characteristics of wounds produced by stargazers. Wounds from the Mediterranean species, *Uranoscopus scaber,* may be fatal.

Treatment: See section on venomous fish stings, pages 158-60.

Prevention: Stargazers should be handled with extreme care in order to avoid being jabbed by the shoulder spines.

Fig. 4-69. **Stargazer** or **Mishmimaokoze**, *Uranoscopus japonicus* Houttuyn. Length 29.6 centimeters (9.7 inches). Inhabits southern Japan, southern Korea, China, Philippine Islands, and Singapore. From Temminck and Schlegel.

Fig. 4-70. **Stargazer**, *Uranoscopus scaber* (Linnaeus). Note the venomous cleithral spine on the shoulder area. This species inhabits the eastern Atlantic Ocean and Mediterranean Sea. Drawing by R.H. Knabenbauer.

Fig. 4-71. *A.* Head of *Uranoscopus scaber*. Note the large spines protruding from the area just above the pectoral fin. Wounds from these spines can be fatal. *B.* Venom apparatus of the **Stargazer**, *Uranoscopus scaber*, showing the left cleithral spine. *C.* Actual fish. The skin has been removed to show the spine. The venom gland is barely visible at the base of the spine. Drawings and photo by R. Kreuzinger.

LEATHERBACK
FAMILY CARANGIDAE

The leatherback, or lae, is a member of the family *Carangidae,* which includes the jacks, scad, and pompanos. A particular characteristic of this family of fishes is the presence of two separate spines in front of the anal fins. Several other species of carangids are believed to possess spines, but the venom apparatus has been described in only the single species *Scomberoides sancti-*

A

B

cleithral
spine

venom
gland

C

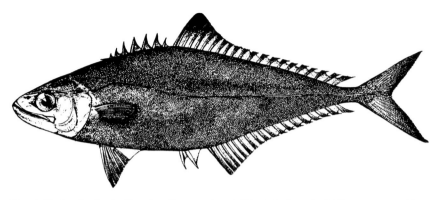

Fig. 4-72. **Leatherback**, *Scomberoides sanctipetri* (Cuvier). Length 64.7 centimeters (25.5 inches). From Fowler.

petri (Cuvier) (fig. 4-72). The leatherback is found throughout the tropical Indo-Pacific region. The carangids are a group of fast-swimming oceanic fishes which are generally encountered in the vicinity of coral reefs and islands.

Venom Apparatus: The venom apparatus consists of seven dorsal spines and two anal spines, their associated musculature, venom glands, and enveloping integumentary sheaths (fig. 4-73).

Medical Aspects: Stings from leatherback spines result in intense pain which may last for several hours. The anal spines are believed to inflict the most serious stings. The wounds are of the puncture-wound variety, and may be accompanied by redness and swelling.

Treatment: See section on venomous fish stings, pages 158-60. There are no specific antidotes available.

Prevention: Handle leatherbacks with care and avoid contact with the spines when removing them from a hook.

TREATMENT OF VENOMOUS FISH STINGS

Efforts in treating venomous fish stings should be directed toward achieving three objectives: (1) alleviating pain, (2) combating effects of the venom, and (3) preventing secondary infection. The pain results from the effects of the trauma produced by the fish spine, venom, and the introduction of slime and other irritating foreign substances into the wound. In the case of stingray and catfish stings, the retrorse (bent backward or downward) barbs of the spine may produce severe lacerations with considerable trauma to the soft tissues. Wounds of this type should be promptly irrigated or washed out with cold salt water or sterile saline if such is available. Fish stings of the

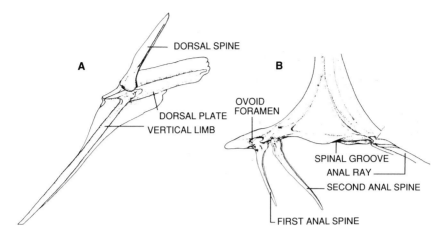

Fig. 4-73. Venom apparatus of the **Leatherback**, *Scomberoides sanctipetri*. A. Dorsal spine. Length of spine 8 millimeters (.3 inch). B. Anal spine. Length of second anal spine 12 millimeters (.4 inch). The venom glands are embedded within the integumentary (skin) sheath surrounding the spines and are not visible to the naked eye. Drawings by S.K. Calloway.

puncture-wound variety are usually small in size, and removal of the poison is more difficult. It may be necessary to make a small incision across the wound, and then apply immediate suction, and possibly irrigation. At any rate, the wound should be sucked promptly in order to remove as much of the venom as possible. However, it should be kept in mind that fishes do not inject their venom in the manner employed by venomous snakes, so at best, results from suction will not be too satisfactory.

The use of a ligature in the treatment of fish stings is of questionable value. Most doctors recommend soaking the injured member in nonscalding hot water for thirty minutes to one hour. The water should be maintained at as high a temperature (120°F or 50°C) as the patient can tolerate without injury, and the treatment should be instituted as soon as possible. If the wound is on the face or body, hot moist compresses should be employed. The heat may have an attenuating effect on the venom, since heating readily destroys fish venoms *in vitro*. Intravenous calcium gluconate injections are sometimes helpful. The addition of magnesium sulfate or epsom salts to the water is believed to be useful. Medical treatment should be administered at a trauma center. Infiltration of the wound area with 0.5–2 percent procaine has been used with good results. If local measures fail to prove satisfactory, intramuscular or intravenous demerol will generally be efficacious. Following the soaking procedure, debridement and further cleansing of the wound may be desirable. Lacerated wounds should be closed with dermal sutures.

If the wound is large, a small drain should be left in it for a day or two. The injured area should be covered with an antiseptic and sterile dressing.

Antibiotic therapy may be required. A course of tetanus antitoxin is an advisable precautionary measure.

The primary shock which follows immediately after the stinging generally responds to simple supportive measures. However, secondary shock resulting from the action of stingray venom on the cardiovascular system requires immediate and vigorous therapy. Treatment should be directed toward maintaining cardiovascular tone and the prevention of any further complications. Respiratory stimulants may also be required.

Stonefish (*Synanceja*) stings are extremely painful and can be lethal. The Commonwealth Serum Laboratories, Melbourne, Australia, have developed an effective antivenin. This antivenin should also be considered for the treatment of envenomations by other scorpionfish species. The antivenin is prepared by hyperimmunizing horses with the stonefish venom. One unit of stonefish antivenin neutralizes 0.01 milligram of stonefish venom (1,000 units will neutralize 10 milligrams of venom). Each stonefish spine produces about 5-10 milligrams of venom.

The initial dose will depend on the number of puncture wounds the patient received, namely,

1-2 punctures—2,000 units (1 ampule)
3-4 punctures—4,000 units (2 ampules)
5-6 punctures—6,000 units (3 ampules)
and so on.

The antivenin should be given by intramuscular injection, but in severe cases it should be given intravenously. If symptoms persist, repeat the initial dosage.

Local infiltration of the wound with emetine hydrochloride (65 milligrams/milliliters) procaine, or potassium permanganate (5 percent), may be helpful in relieving the pain, but generally soaking the limb in hot water is effective. Stonefish antivenin is produced in ampules of 2,000 units (approximately 2 milliliters). The antivenin should be stored, protected from light, at 40-60°F or 2-8°C.

SEA SNAKES
FAMILY HYDROPHIIDAE

Sea snakes are aquatic inhabitants of the tropical Pacific and Indian Oceans, ranging for the most part from the Samoan Islands westward to the East

Coast of Africa, from Japan to the Persian Gulf, along the coasts of Asia, through Indo-Australian seas to Australia. One species, *Pelamis platurus*, has an enormous geographical range extending from the west coast of Latin America across the Pacific and Indian Oceans to the east coast of Africa, and from southern Siberia to Tasmania. With the exception of a single freshwater species, *Hydrophis semperi*, which lives in freshwater Lake Bombon (also called Lake Taal), Luzon, Philippine Islands, all are marine. *Laticauda crockeri* is limited to the brackish water of Lake Tungano, Rennel Island, Solomon Islands. There are about fifty known species of sea snakes.

Sea snakes generally prefer sheltered coastal waters and are particularly fond of river mouths. Around shore, sea snakes may inhabit rock crevices, tree roots, coral boulders, or pilings. In regions where sea snakes are plentiful, more than one hundred snakes may be taken by fishermen in a single net haul. A factor governing the distribution of most sea snakes seems to be the depth of water in which they feed. The depth must be shallow enough for them to go to the bottom to feed and to rise to the surface for air. However, sea snakes have been observed 160.9 to 241.4 kilometers (100 to 150 miles) from land. A large group of Stokes's sea snake (*Astrotia stokesi*) was once observed migrating between the Malay Peninsula and Sumatra. The mass of snakes was estimated to be about 3.1 meters (10 feet) wide and at least 96.5 kilometers (60 miles) long, consisting of several million individuals. Sea snakes are said to be the most abundant of all the reptiles.

With their compressed, oarlike tails, sea snakes are well adapted for locomotion in the marine environment. Swimming is accomplished by lateral undulatory movements of the body. Sea snakes are able to float, lying motionless for long periods of time. They are also able to move backward or forward with amazing rapidity, but when placed on land, are very awkward and move about with difficulty.

The bodies of sea snakes are covered with scales and have no limbs, ear openings, sternum, or urinary bladder, and are more or less compressed posteriorly with a flat, paddle-shaped tail. Their eyes are immobile, covered by transparent scales, and are without lids. The tongue is slender, forked, and protrusile. Sea snakes are equipped with a well-developed venom apparatus.

Sea snakes are able to remain submerged for hours, but are unable to utilize oxygen from the water as fish do. They are equipped with an extended right lung, but the left lung is either vestigial or absent. Sea snakes capture their food underwater, usually swallowing the fish head first. They feed on or near the bottom, around rocks, holes, or crevices where they capture eels and other small fishes, which are promptly killed with a vigorous bite of their venomous jaws.

The disposition of sea snakes is a subject of controversy, but of practical importance to those coming in contact with them. After reviewing the experiences of numerous writers and divers, one can only conclude that the docility of a sea snake varies with the species, the season of the year, and the manner in which the snake is approached. Generally speaking, sea snakes tend to be docile, but under some circumstances may be quite aggressive. One should not become overconfident and should always be aware that a set of fully functional fangs and an extremely virulent venom (more toxic than king cobra venom) accompanies an apparent gentle nature. Bites are usually contracted while handling nets, sorting fish, wading, washing, or accidentally stepping on the snakes. Most species of sea snakes are .9-1.2 meters (3-4 feet long) but may attain a length of 2.7 meters (9 feet) or more. There are about fifty different species of sea snakes. The following species are reputed to be particularly dangerous to man.

SEA SNAKE, *Enhydrina schistosa* (Daudin) (fig. 4-74). Inhabits the Persian Gulf to Cochin China, and north coast of Australia.

CHITTUL, or BANDED SEA SNAKE, *Hydrophis caerulescens* (Shaw) (fig. 4-75). Ranges from Persian Gulf to Japan, and the Malay Archipelago.

SEA SNAKE, *Hydrophis nigrocinctus* (Daudin) (fig. 4-76). Inhabits the Bay of Bengal.

HARDWICK'S SEA SNAKE, *Lapemis hardwickii* Gray (fig. 4-77). Ranges from southern Japan to the Merguri Archipelago, and along the coast of northern Australia.

YELLOW-BELLIED SEA SNAKE, *Pelamis platurus* (Linnaeus) (fig. 4-78). This species has the greatest range of any sea snake, extending from East Africa, throughout the Indo-Australian area, eastward to the Gulf of Panama.

Venom Apparatus: Sea snakes inflict their wounds with the use of fangs, which are reduced in size, but are of the cobra type (fig. 4-79). In comparison with other venomous snakes, sea snake dentition is relatively feeble but, nevertheless, fully developed for venom conduction. The venom apparatus consists of the venom glands and fangs. The venom glands are situated, one on either side, behind and below the eye, and in front of the tympanic bones. They are ovate and have an elongated venom duct, which terminates at the base of the fangs. Most sea snakes have two fangs on each side but some have only one. The venom duct enters at the base of the fang through a relatively broad, triangular opening of the canal. Sea snake venom has neurotoxic, myotoxic, and hemotoxic properties. One drop (.03 milliliters) contains sufficient poison to kill three adult men. Some species can inject up to eight drops in a single bite. It should be noted that because of the small size of the fangs, a bite does not always result in an envenomation.

Medical Aspects: Symptoms caused by the bite of a sea snake characteristically develop rather slowly, taking from twenty minutes to several hours, but usually about one hour, before definite symptoms begin. Aside from the initial prick, there is no pain or reaction at the site of the bite. The victim may even fail to connect the bite with his illness.

In some instances, the initial generalized symptoms are a mild euphoria, whereas in others there is aching and anxiety. A sensation of thickening of the tongue and a generalized feeling of stiffness of the muscles gradually develops. Common complaints during the early stage are "aching," "stiffness," or pain upon movement. There may be little indication of actual weakness at this time. The paralysis that soon follows is usually generalized, but of the ascending type, beginning with the legs, and, within an hour or two, involving the trunk, arms, and neck muscles. Lockjaw is one of the outstanding symptoms. Drooping of the eyelids is an early and characteristic sign. The pulse becomes weak, irregular, and pupils dilate. Speaking and swallowing become increasingly difficult. Thirst, burning, or dryness of the throat may also be present. Nausea and vomiting are not uncommon. Muscle twitchings, twisting movements, and spasms have been noted. Ocular and

Fig. 4-74. **Sea Snake,** *Enhydrina schistosa* (Daudin). Painting by R.H. Knabenbauer.

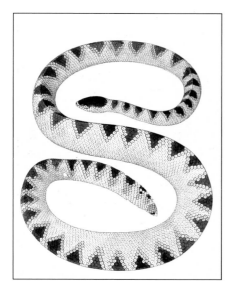

Fig. 4-75. **Chittul** or **Banded Sea Snake**, *Hydrophis caerulescens* (Shaw). Painting by M. Shirao.

Fig. 4-76. **Sea Snake**, *Hydrophis nigrocinctus* (Daudin). Painting by M. Shirao.

facial paralysis may later develop. In severe intoxication, the symptoms become progressively more intense, the skin of the patient is cold, clammy, cyanotic, convulsions begin and are frequent, respiratory distress becomes very pronounced, and finally the victim succumbs in an unconscious state. The overall case fatality rate has been estimated to be about 28 percent.

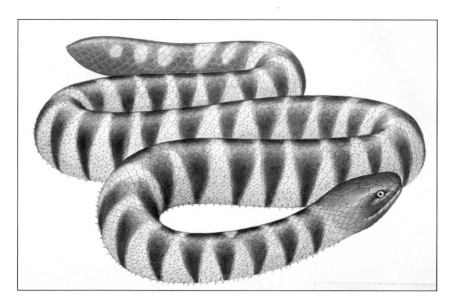

Fig. 4-77. **Hardwick's Sea Snake**, *Lapemis hardwickii* Gray. Painting by M. Shirao.

Fig. 4-78. **Yellow-bellied Sea Snake**, *Pelamis platurus* (Linnaeus). Drawing by M. Shirao.

Treatment: If treatment is to be effective it must be instituted immediately following the bite. First aid and treatment should generally be directed toward:

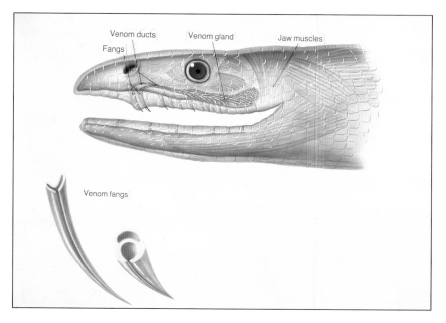

Fig. 4-79. Venom apparatus of sea snake. The fangs are hollow with an open groove throughout most of their length. L. Barlow, after West.

1. Removing as much venom as possible from the wound;
2. Retarding absorption of the venom;
3. Neutralizing the venom;
4. Mitigating the effects produced by the venom; and
5. Preventing complications, including secondary infections.

First Aid: Absorption of sea snake venom is rapid. In most instances the venom is absorbed before first aid can be administered. Suction is of value only if it can be applied within the first few minutes following the bite. It is generally advisable to leave the bite alone. The affected limb should be immediately immobilized, and *all exertion must be avoided*. The patient should lie down and keep the immobilized part below the level of the heart. A tourniquet should be applied tight enough to occlude the superficial venous and lymphatic return. The tourniquet should be applied to the thigh in leg bites or above the elbow in upper limb bites. It should be released for ninety seconds every ten minutes. A tourniquet is of little value if applied later than thirty minutes following the bite, and it should not be used for more than four hours. The tourniquet should be removed as soon as anti-venin therapy has been started. Some venomologists believe that the tourniquet is of little or no value in sea snake bites. If sea snake antivenin, or a polyvalent antivenin containing a krait (*Elapidae*) fraction is available, it should be administered intramuscularly either in the buttocks or at some other site distant from the bite. The antivenin should be given only after the appropriate skin or conjunctival test has been made. There appears to be an increasing number of physicians who recommend injecting the antivenin in adequate quantities intravenously without concern for side reactions. They believe that any hypersensitivity can be controlled with the use of adrenalin. Usually one unit (vial or ampule) is sufficient until the patient can be transported to a physician. Keep the patient warm. The patient should not be given alcoholic beverages but may be given water, coffee, or tea. Keep the patient calm and reassured with encouraging words and actions. Transport the patient immediately to the nearest doctor or hospital but do not allow him to walk or exert himself in any way. If at all possible place the offending dead snake in a container and give it to the physician for identification.

Therapy: Sea snake envenomation is a medical emergency requiring immediate attention. A delay in instituting proper medical treatment can lead to consequences far more tragic than might be incurred in an ordinary traumatic injury. The first step is to determine if envenomation has actually occurred. In most instances, by the time the patient reaches the physician, the one-hour test period since the bite was made will have been exceeded so there should be some clinical evidence of poisoning if any is to develop. If the patient has been carefully examined and there is no evidence of intoxication, the patient needs only reassurance and observation for a period of an hour or two. If after a period of observation there is no evidence of toxemia, the patient can be released.

If a period of more than one hour has elapsed and there is definite evidence of intoxication, antivenin therapy should be instituted immediately upon arrival at the hospital or physician's office. At this time, suction and incision are useless. There is now available a sea snake antivenin, which is prepared from the venom of *Enhydrina schistosa* and can be obtained from the Commonwealth Serum Laboratories, Melbourne, Australia, and the Snake and Venom Research Laboratories, Penang, Malaysia. This antivenin is concentrated and purified so as to minimize hypersensitivity reactions. If sea snake antivenin is not available, use a polyvalent antiserum containing a krait (*Elapidae*) fraction. A skin or conjunctival test should be done prior to injection of the antivenin. In persons with a history of extensive allergies, the antivenin should be injected with caution even in the presence of a negative skin test. Follow the instructions given in the brochure that

accompanies the antivenin. If instructions are not available, these procedures can be used: The antivenin can be given either intramuscularly or
intravenously. The intramuscular route is said to be safer, but less effective.
Again, physicians are increasingly recommending injecting the antivenin
intravenously without concern for hypersensitivity. A portion of the first
ampule should be injected subcutaneously proximal to the bite, surrounding
the wound, or in advance of the swelling. Antivenin should never be injected
into the injured part. A second portion of the antivenin should be injected
intramuscularly into a large muscle mass at some distance from the bite, and
the last portion should be given intravenously.

Intravenous antivenin is indicated with patients in shock. When given
intravenously the antivenin should be administered by the drip method over
a period of one hour. The antivenin can be added to the physiological saline
solution and given in a continuous drip. Subsequent doses can then be added
to the saline solution.

The incidence of sensitivity reactions is said to be lessened when the
antivenin is combined with hyaluronidase (10 milliliters of antivenin with
1,000 units of hyaluronidase) and given intramuscularly. It is recommended
that an injection of 250 milligrams of cortisone be given intramuscularly
prior to administering the antivenin, but not at the same time that the antivenin is given. If hypersensitivity reactions occur, they can usually be controlled with adrenalin subcutaneously with or without intravenous antihistaminic drugs. If the patient shows a positive reaction to the initial sensitivity
test, the antivenin will have to be administered in graded doses in accordance
with standard medical procedures for desensitization.

One ampule of sea snake antivenin neutralizes 10 milligrams of *Enhydrina schistosa* venom and the venom of other common sea snake species.
The minimum effective dosage is 1 ampule. In severe poisoning as evidenced
by ptosis, weakness of external eye muscles, dilation of pupils with sluggish
light reaction, and leucocytosis exceeding 20,000, 3 to 4 or more ampules
are required. Children generally respond satisfactorily to smaller doses of
antivenin than that required by adults, contrary to previous textbook state-
ments. If envenomation is present, antivenin therapy should be given as soon
as possible, but it may be successful even eight or more hours after the bite
has occurred. Parenteral fluids should always be given following a severe
envenomation. Cryotherapy is not recommended.

Supportive measures such as blood transfusions, plasma, vasopressor
drugs, antibiotics, antitetanus agents, oxygen, etc., may be required. Corticosteroids are the drugs of choice in combating delayed allergic reactions

provoked by the venom or the horse serum. Neurological disorders such as cerebral, meningeal, myelitic, radicular, and neuritic disorders (particularly of the fifth and sixth cervical roots) have been reported. Delayed reactions usually do not appear until three to seven days after administration of the antivenin.

Sensitivity Tests: A sensitivity test must be carried out on all victims of sea snake poisoning before horse serum antivenin is administered. Directions for these tests will usually be found in the package containing the antivenin. In the absence of specific instructions, follow these steps:

1. Inject 0.10 milliliters of a 1:10 dilution of the horse serum or antivenin intracutaneously on the inner surface of the forearm. Use the specific hypodermic needle provided for the test. If one is not provided, use a short, 27-gauge needle. If the test is done correctly, a wheal will be raised at the site of the injection. The wheal is white at first, but if the test is positive, the area about the point of injection will become red within ten to fifteen minutes. If any local or systemic allergic manifestations develop within twenty minutes of the test, do not give antivenin. Leave this decision to the physician.

If the patient develops a severe reaction to the test (restlessness, flushing, sneezing, urticaria, swelling of the eyelids and lips, respiratory distress, or cyanosis), inject 0.3 to 0.5 milliliters of 1:1,000 adrenalin subcutaneously and observe the patient closely. Be prepared to administer artificial respiration. A cardiac stimulant may also be needed if shock develops.

2. An alternative to the skin test is the eye test. One or two drops of a 1:10 solution of the horse serum or antivenin are placed on the conjunctiva of one eye. If the test is positive, redness of the conjunctiva will develop within a few minutes. If the reaction is very severe, it should be controlled by depositing a drop or two of 1:1,000 adrenalin directly on the conjunctiva.

3. If a serum sensitivity test is positive, desensitization should be carried out before administering antivenin.

Prevention: Although sea snakes are generally considered to be docile and at times reluctant to bite, some species are aggressive and have no biting inhibitions. It should be kept in mind that even the "harmless" snakes are fully equipped with venom apparatus and a potentially lethal poison. Sea snakes thus merit respect and thoughtful consideration. Sea snakes may occasionally bite a bather. It is estimated that one sea snake bite occurs per 270,000 man-bathing-hours in an endemic area such as Penang, Malaysia.

The most dangerous areas in which to swim are river mouths. It is probable that accidents are more likely to occur in a river mouth where the sea snakes are more numerous and the water more turbid. The turbidity of the water and resulting poor visibility for the sea snake may contribute to their becoming fearless and less discriminating in their biting habits. When possible, avoid swimming in a river mouth. When wading in an area inhabited by sea snakes, shuffle your feet. This will prevent stepping on them. The majority of sea snake bites have taken place among native fishermen removing fish from their nets. A person should be extremely careful in handling a net haul containing sea snakes. It is advisable first to remove the snakes with the use of a hooked stick or wire before attempting to handle them. Sea snakes are occasionally captured while fishing with a hook and line. Do not attempt to remove the hook from the mouth of the snake. Cut the line, and let the snake drop into the water. *Do not handle the snake.*

CHAPTER 5

MARINE ANIMALS POISONOUS TO EAT: INVERTEBRATES

Tropical waters attract the skin diver who is seeking new adventure. The waters are warm and clear, and the sealife is abundant. But venturing into strange tropical waters is not without some danger. In this chapter we are not concerned about what might harm us from without, but rather from the dangers within—those seafoods likely to be eaten by the diver while in the field. Fortunately, most seafoods are edible and nourishing. However, there are those known to contain some of the most toxic food poisons known to science. These illnesses are not due to bacterial food poisoning, but to a group of marine animals whose flesh, under certain circumstances, may contain poisonous chemical substances.

CLASSIFICATION OF POISONOUS MARINE ANIMALS

A large number of poisonous marine animals are known to marine biotoxicologists, but only a few general categories of them will be dealt with here. For the purposes of this book, marine animals that are poisonous to eat may be classified as follows:

POISONOUS INVERTEBRATES

A. Molluscs which have been feeding on toxic dinoflagellates can, if ingested, cause paralytic shellfish poisoning.
B. Coelenterates.
   1. Sea anemones (*Rhodactis*).
   2. Zoanthids (*Palythoa*).
C. Echinoderms.
   1. Sea urchin eggs.
   2. Sea cucumbers.
D. Arthropods.

171

1. Asiatic horseshoe crabs.
2. Tropical reef crabs.

POISONOUS VERTEBRATES

A. FISHES. There are estimated to be more than four hundred species of fishes that can produce an intoxication when ingested. Intoxication resulting from the ingestion of fish flesh is referred to as *ichthyosarcotoxism*. There are various types of *ichthyosarcotoxism*, but only a few of the more common poisonings will be presented in this manual. They include the following:

    1. *Elasmobranch poisoning*—due to the ingestion of poisonous sharks, rays, and some of their relatives.

    2. *Ciguatera*—due to the ingestion of various species of tropical reef fishes. A related form of poisoning is known as *clupeotoxism*, which is due to the ingestion of herringlike fishes of the Order Clupeiformes.

    3. *Scombroid poisoning*—due to the ingestion of inadequately preserved tunas and related species of scombroid fishes.

    4. *Gempylid poisoning*—due to the ingestion of the castor oil or gempylid fish.

    5. *Hallucinogenic fish poisoning*—due to ingestion of certain tropical reef fishes that produce hallucinations.

    6. *Puffer poisoning*—due to the eating of the flesh of puffer fishes, members of the Order Tetraodontiformes.

B. REPTILES. Some of the most violent marine biotoxications known have been caused by the eating of the flesh of marine turtles of the genera *Chelonia, Eretmochelys,* and *Dermochelys.*

C. MARINE MAMMALS. Ingestion of the flesh and various organs of certain marine mammals may cause violent intoxications. This group includes the polar bear, certain whales, dolphins, porpoises, and sea lions.

    Each of these groups of poisonous marine organisms will be discussed in greater detail in the two chapters that follow.

POISONOUS MARINE INVERTEBRATES
PARALYTIC SHELLFISH POISONING

Paralytic shellfish poisoning occurs in human beings as a result of eating molluscs containing potent biotoxins derived from planktonic unicellular organisms known as dinoflagellates. These dinoflagellates are sometimes observed to "bloom" in vast numbers and may cause a phenomenon which

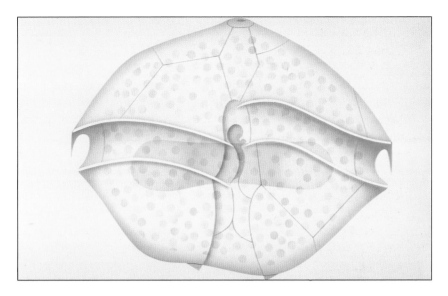

Fig. 5-1. *Gonyaulax catenella* Whedon and Kofoid. ×1440. Painting by R. Kreuzinger.

is referred to as "red tide." At times red tide may cause a mass mortality of fishes. However, molluscs may become poisonous from feeding on dinoflagellates even when a red tide is not in evidence. Dinoflagellate blooms constitute a public health hazard because of their unpredictability and the rapidity with which toxic concentrations may develop. The precise cause of these blooms has not been fully determined.

There are many different kinds of dinoflagellates, but only about five species appear to be most commonly involved and of concern to human health. These dinoflagellates bloom sporadically throughout the world, but seem to occur most frequently in north and south temperate latitudes. There are two species of dinoflagellates most commonly incriminated in human intoxications: *Gonyaulax*[1] *catenella* Whedon and Kofoid (figs. 5-1, 5-5), along the north Pacific coast of North America from central California; northward along the coasts of Oregon, Washington, British Columbia, Alaska; and westward along the Aleutian Islands to the coasts of Japan; and in the Southern Hemisphere along the coast of Chile; *Gonyaulax tamarensis*[2] Lebour (figs. 5-2, 5-5), the most common toxic dinoflagellate along the northeast coast of North America including Massachusetts, New Hampshire,

[1] The genus *Gonyaulax* has also been designated as *Protogonyaulax*.
[2] According to some investigators, *G. tamarensis* is actually nontoxic, and the correct identification is *G. excavata* Braarud.

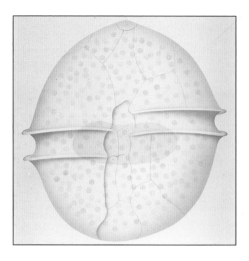

Fig. 5-2. *Gonyaulax tamarensis* Lebour.
×1200. Painting by R. Kreuzinger.

and Maine; and in Canada along the coasts of Nova Scotia, New Brunswick, and Quebec; and across the Atlantic Ocean to the North Sea countries of Britain, West Germany, Belgium, and Denmark. *Pyrodinium phoneus* Woloszynska and Conrad[3] (fig. 5-3) has been incriminated in the Netherlands. *Dinophysis* spp. have caused diarrhetic shellfish poisoning in Japan. *G. Catenella* (fig. 5-5) is also a toxic species. Another dinoflagellate which is known to be toxic and may cause mass mortality among fishes but may or may not be involved in human biotoxications, is *Gymnodinium breve*[4] Davis (fig. 5-4). *Gamberdiscus toxicus* Adachi and Fukuyo has been incriminated as a causative agent of ciguatera fish poisoning. (See Chapter 6).

Numerous different types of dinoflagellate poisons are now known to exist. They may vary in quantity and in type within a single species of dinoflagellate and the molluscs ingesting them. The chemistry of these poisons will not be discussed.

The number of toxic dinoflagellates in the water varies according to the season of the year and the abundance of nutrient chemical substances that are available in the water. Over a period of time, it has been observed that the dangerous part of the year when dinoflagellates multiply is the warm season, which varies somewhat, but in north temperate regions is from March to November. An exception to this rule is the Alaskan butter clam, *Saxidomus giganteus* (Deshayes), which may have dangerous toxicity levels in certain coastal areas of Alaska at almost any time of the year.

[3] *P. phoneus* is now considered to be *Gonyaulax phoneus*.
[4] *Gymnodinium* has been designated as *Ptychodiscus*.

Fig. 5-3. *Pyrodinium phoneus* Woloszynska and Conrad. ×1980. These are the most commonly encountered dinoflagellates causing paralytic shellfish poisoning. *Pyrodinium phoneus* is now considered to be *Gonyaulax phoneus*. Painting by R. Kreuzinger.

SHELLFISH MOST COMMONLY INVOLVED IN HUMAN POISONING

FAMILY CARDIIDAE

COMMON COCKLE, *Cardium edule* Linnaeus (fig. 5-6). Inhabits European Seas.

FAMILY DONACIDAE

WHITE MUSSEL, *Donax serra* (Chemnitz)(fig. 5-6). Inhabits South Africa.

FAMILY MACTRIDAE

SOLID SURF CLAM, *Spisula solidissima* (Dillwyn)(fig. 5-6). Occurs from Labrador to North Carolina.

GAPER or SUMMER CLAM, *Schizothaerus nuttalli* (Conrad)(fig. 5-6). Found from Prince William Sound, Alaska, south to Scammons Lagoon, Baja California, and northern Japan.

FAMILY MYACIDAE

SOFT-SHELLED CLAM, *Mya arenaria* Linnaeus (fig. 5-7). Inhabits Britain, Scandinavia, Greenland, Atlantic coast of North America, south to

Fig. 5-4. D. *Gymnodinium breve* Davis. ×1440. This dinoflagellate may cause red tide and a mass mortality of fishes. It may also cause respiratory irritation in humans. Painting by R. Kreuzinger.

the Carolinas; Alaska, south to Japan, and Vancouver, British Columbia; California and Oregon coasts.

FAMILY MYTILIDAE

COMMON MUSSEL, *Mytilus californianus* Conrad (fig. 5-7). Inhabits Unalaska, Aleutian Islands, eastward and southward to Socorro Island.

BAY MUSSEL, *Mytilus edulis* Linnaeus (fig. 5-7). Ranges from the Arctic Ocean to South Carolina, Alaska to Cape San Lucas, Baja California; practically worldwide in temperate waters.

NORTHERN HORSE MUSSEL, *Modiolus modiolus* (Linnaeus)(fig. 5-7). Found along the Pacific Coast of America from the Arctic Ocean to San Ignacio Lagoon, Baja California; circumboreal.

FAMILY SOLENIDAE

ATLANTIC JACKKNIFE or RAZOR CLAM, *Ensis directus* Conrad (fig. 5-8). Ranges from the Gulf of St. Lawrence River to Florida.

FAMILY VENERIDAE

ALASKAN BUTTER CLAM, SMOOTH WASHINGTON or BUTTER CLAM, *Saxidomus giganteus* (Deshayes)(fig. 5-8). Ranges from Sitka, Alaska, to San Francisco Bay, California.

Fig. 5-5. **Other Dinoflagellates.** *A. Gonyaulax catenella* Whedon and Kofoid, isolated from a red tide sample collected January, 1975, from Owasa Bay, Mie Prefecture, Japan. Dorsal view of a two-celled chain. ×1440. *B. Gonyaulax tamarensis* Lebour, isolated from Lynher River, England, collected June, 1957. Ventral view with cells right side more exposed. The toxicity of this species has been questioned. ×2200. *C. Gonyaulax excavata* (Braarud), isolated from a red tide from Lanesville Station, Gloucester, Massachusetts. This is now believed to be the toxic causative agent of the New England red tide rather than *Gonyaulax tamarensis*. ×1200. *D. Gonyaulax acatenella* Whedon and Kofoid, isolated from a red tide sample from Malaspina Inlet, British Colombia, Canada. Taken in June, 1965. Reputed to be toxic. ×1700. Electronic scanning micrograph courtesy of A.R. Loeblich, III, and L.A. Loeblich.

B

D

A

C

Fig. 5-6. A. **Common Cockle**, *Cardium edule* Linnaeus. × 1.1 Inhabits European seas. B. **White Mussel**, *Donax serra* (Chemnitz). × 0.7 Inhabits South Africa. C. **Solid Surf Clam**, *Spisula solidissima* (Dillwyn). × 0.4 Occurs from Labrador to North Carolina. D. **Gaper** or **Summer Clam**, *Schizothaerus nuttalli* (Conrad). × 0.2 Found from Prince William Sound, Alaska, south to Scammons Lagoon, Baja California, and northern Japan. Photos by R. Kreuzinger, courtesy S.S. Berry.

Fig. 5-7. A. **Soft-Shelled Clam**, *Mya arenaria* Linnaeus. × 0.2 Inhabits Britain, Scandinavia, Greenland, Atlantic coast of North America, south to Carolina; Alaska, south to Japan, and Vancouver, British Columbia; California and Oregon coasts. B. **Common Mussel**, *Mytilus californianus* Conrad. × 0.3 Inhabits Unalaska, Aleutian Islands, eastward and southward to Socorro Island. C. **Bay Mussel**, *Mytilus edulis* Linnaeus. × 0.9 Ranges from the Arctic Ocean to South Carolina, Alaska to Cape San Lucas, Baja California; practically worldwide in temperate waters. D. **Northern Horse Mussel**, *Modiolus modiolus* (Linnaeus). × 0.4 Found along the Pacific Coast of America from the Arctic Ocean to San Ignacio Lagoon, Baja California; circumboreal. Photos by R. Kreuzinger, courtesy S.S. Berry.

COMMON WASHINGTON or BUTTER CLAM, *Saxidomus nuttalli* Conrad (fig. 5-8). Ranges from Humbolt Bay, California to San Quentin Bay, Baja California.

Medical Aspects: Three types of shellfish poisoning are recognized by physicians:

1. *Gastrointestinal type*—characterized by such symptoms as nausea, vomiting, diarrhea, and abdominal pain. This type usually develops about ten to twelve hours after eating shellfish, and is believed to be caused by bacterial contamination.
2. *Allergic type*—characterized by redness of the skin, swelling development of a hivelike rash, itching, headache, nasal congestion, abdominal pain, dryness of the throat, swelling of the tongue, palpitation of the heart, and difficulty in breathing. This type probably results from a sensitivity to shellfish on the part of the individual.
3. *Paralytic type*—this last type is caused specifically by the dinoflagellate poison present in shellfish. The disease has also been termed paralytic shellfish poisoning (PSP). The early symptoms are a tingling or burning sensation of the lips, gums, tongue, and face, which gradually spreads elsewhere to the body. The tingling areas later become numb, and movements of the muscles of the body may become very difficult. Other symptoms frequently present are weakness, dizziness, joint aches, increased salivation, intense thirst, and difficulty in swallowing. Nausea, vomiting, diarrhea, and abdominal pain are relatively rare. The muscular paralysis may become increasingly severe until death ensues.

Inhalation of toxic products contained in windblown spray from red tide areas of *Gymnodinium breve* may cause irritation of the mucous membranes of the nose and throat, resulting in coughing, sneezing, and respiratory distress.

Treatment: There is no specific treatment available for paralytic shellfish poisoning and no known antidotes. Evacuation of the gastrointestinal tract should be instituted as soon as possible if shellfish have been ingested.

Fig. 5-8. *A.* **Atlantic Jackknife** or **Razor Clam,** *Ensis directus* Conrad. × 0.3 Ranges from the Gulf of St. Lawrence River to Florida. *B.* **Alaskan Butter Clam, Smooth Washington** or **Butter Clam,** *Saxidomus giganteus* (Deshayes). × 0.7 Ranges from Sitka, Alaska, to San Francisco Bay, California. *C.* **Common Washington Clam,** *Saxidomus nuttalli* Conrad. × 0.3 Ranges from Humboldt Bay, California to San Quentin, Bay, Baja California. Photos by R. Kreuzinger, courtesy S.S. Berry.

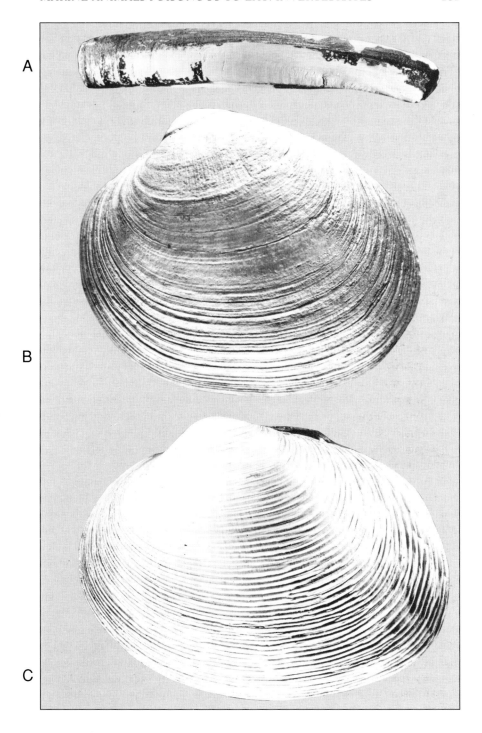

Vomiting can be stimulated by swallowing large quantities of salt water, egg white, or by merely placing one's finger down the throat. Alkaline fluids, such as a solution of ordinary baking soda are said to be of value, since the poison is rapidly destroyed by these fluids. Artificial respiration may be required. See a physician at once if you are fortunate enough to be near one.

Prevention: The extremely toxic nature of this poison cannot be over-emphasized. Most areas where paralytic shellfish poisoning is likely to occur are monitored by local public health authorities. When toxic shellfish are discovered, the area is placed under quarantine. One should adhere strictly to local quarantine regulations. Since poisonous shellfish cannot be detected by their appearance, smell, or by discoloration of a silver object or garlic placed in cooking water, etc., it is only by careful scientific laboratory procedures that paralytic shellfish poison can be determined with any degree of certainty.

The digestive organs, or dark meat, gills, and in some shellfish species the siphon, contain the greatest concentration of the poison (fig. 5-9). The musculature or white meat is generally harmless; however, it should be thoroughly washed before cooking. The broth, or bouillon, in which the shellfish is boiled is especially dangerous since the poison is water soluble. The broth should be discarded if there is the slightest doubt. The tidal location from which the shellfish were gathered cannot be used as a criterion for whether the shellfish are safe to eat. Poisonous shellfish may be found in either low or high tidal zones. If in doubt—throw them out!

COELENTERATE POISONING

Poisoning from coelenterates is of two types, namely:

1. Accidental swallowing of jellyfish tentacles. If a tentacle fragment containing nematocysts is ingested (usually by curious children), an intraoral envenomation may occur. This is extremely painful and may cause rapid swelling of the lips, tongue, and soft tissues of the pharynx and hypopharynx, leading to airway obstruction. The airway should be rapidly assessed for obstruction, a dangerous situation which may be recognized by marked swelling, drooling, change in voice, difficult

Fig. 5-9. Internal anatomy of shellfish, showing parts of the body likely to contain paralytic ▶ shellfish poison. A. **Mussel,** *Mytilus.* Liver and intestines (dark meat) and gills are the most dangerous parts to eat. B. **Alaska Butter Clam,** *Saxidomus.* The poison is concentrated primarily in the siphon. Photos by R. Kreuzinger, courtesy S.S. Berry.

ANTERIOR ADDUCTOR MUSCLE

POSTERIOR ADDUCTOR MUSCLE

LIVER AND INTESTINES

A

FOOT   BYSSUS   GILLS

ANTERIOR ADDUCTOR MUSCLE
REMOVED

LIVER

POSTERIOR ADDUCTOR MUSCLE

INTESTINES

B

SIPHON

FOOT   MANTLE EDGE

breathing, cyanosis, and agitation. In such case, the rapid placement of an endotracheal tube directly through the vocal cords maintains the airway and allows the victim to breathe through such an unpleasant episode. Under no circumstances should anything be given to the victim for a mouthwash or gargle unless he is alert, breathing freely, and capable of unrestricted, purposeful swallowing.

2. Ingestion of poisonous sea anemones. Intoxication from the ingestion of poisonous sea anemones is rare, but occasionally occurs in the tropical Pacific. Most poisonings occur in children who eat raw sea anemones.

Sea anemones are commonly eaten by the natives of Samoa, but only certain species, and, only after the anemones are cooked. *Rhodactis howesi* Kent (fig. 5-10), known locally as *matalelei*, and *Physobrachia douglasi* Kent (fig. 5-10), known locally as *lumane*, are generally considered to be poisonous when raw, but safe to eat when cooked. *Radianthus paumotensis* (Dana) (fig. 5-10), known locally as *Matamala samasama*, is considered to be poisonous both raw and cooked.

Medical Aspects: Initial symptoms are those of acute gastritis including nausea, vomiting, abdominal pain, cyanosis, and prostration. Shortly after ingestion the victim may become stuporous with an absence of superficial reflexes, but with a normal pulse rate and blood pressure. Eventually the patient may go into prolonged shock and die with a pulmonary edema.

The accidental ingestion of jellyfish tentacles is most likely to occur as a result of swallowing seawater in a region where there has been a recent storm. During stormy weather, jellyfish tentacles may be torn from the animal and are found floating loose in the water. Accidental swallowing of seawater may thereby result in ingestion of tentacles and cause an intraoral envenomation. One should be aware of the danger of swallowing seawater under these conditions.

Prevention: Ingestion of raw tropical sea anemone species should be avoided.

Treatment: Symptomatic, no known specific antidote.

POISONOUS ZOANTHIDS

Some of the zoanthids, or soft-corals, of the genus *Palythoa* have been found to contain one of the most deadly poisons known to marine biotoxicologists. This poison is produced within the body of the organism rather than in the

Fig. 5-10. **Poisonous Sea Anemones**. *Top left, Radianthus paumotensis* (Dana). Diameter up to 7.6 centimeters (3 inches). *Top right, Physobrachia douglasi* Kent. Diameter up to 5.1 centimeters (2 inches). *Middle, Rhodactis howesi* Kent. Diameter about 6.4 centimeters (2.5 inches). *Bottom left, Palythoa toxica* Walsh and Bowers. Diameter of disk 7.6 millimeters (3 inches). *Bottom right, Palythoa tuberculosa* Esper. Diameter of disk 7.6 millimeters (3 inches). Paintings by R.H. Knabenbauer.

stinging nematocysts of the tentacles. The poison, designated "palytoxin," has been demonstrated to have a potent action on the nervous and muscular systems of experimental animals (crabs and mice), but little is known concerning the effects of palytoxin in humans. The poison can be inactivated with heat and acids, and is probably destroyed by gastric juices. When swimming in closed tidal pools containing large numbers of *Palythoa,* a person may develop sensations of numbness and tingling of the lips and mouth.

Species of the soft-coral *Palythoa* are found both in the Caribbean and the tropical Pacific. In the Hawaiian Islands *Palythoa* is referred to as the "deadly seaweed of Hana (Limu-Make O Hana)." *Palythoa* (See fig. 5-10 on page 185) are generally found growing in tidal pools or other shallow water protected areas, and may be encrusted on shells, seaweed, corals, or rocks.

Persons working for prolonged periods in confined tidal pools inhabited by this coelenterate should do so with caution. One should keep in mind that palytoxin is extremely poisonous and may cause serious skin reactions to sensitive persons. Contact with the slime of *Palythoa* in an open wound may cause malaise, muscle cramps, abdominal pain, immune dysfunction, and could be fatal. Handle this sea anemone with extreme care.

POISONOUS ECHINODERMS

There are relatively few echinoderms (starfishes, sea urchins, sea cucumbers) known to produce human oral intoxications. Only two groups have been incriminated to any significant extent, namely:

SEA URCHIN EGGS. Reports have appeared from time to time of poisonings due to the ingestion of sea urchin eggs. The EUROPEAN SEA URCHIN, *Paracentrotus lividus* Lamarck (fig. 5-11), inhabiting the Atlantic coasts of Europe and the Mediterranean, and the WHITE SEA URCHIN, *Tripneustes ventricosus* (Lamarck) (fig. 5-12), inhabiting the West Indies, have been incriminated. It is believed that the poison is contracted from algae upon which the sea urchins feed.

Poisonings usually occur during the reproductive season of the year. Symptoms consist of an acute gastritis, nausea, vomiting, diarrhea, abdominal pain, and severe migrainelike headaches. Little else is known about sea urchin poisoning in humans, or the nature of the poison.

SEA CUCUMBERS. These are a group of sluggish creatures that move over the bottom of the sea by means of rhythmic contractions of a sausage-like body. They have a series of tentacles circling the mouth at the anterior end of the body (fig. 5-13). Sea cucumbers, members of the class Holothuroidea, serve as important items of food in some parts of the world where they are sold under the name of "Trepang" or "bêche-de-mer." They are boiled and then dried in the sun or smoked. "Trepang" is used to flavor soups and stews.

Contact with liquid ejected from the visceral cavity of some sea cucumber species may result in dermatitis or blindness. The poison of sea cucum-

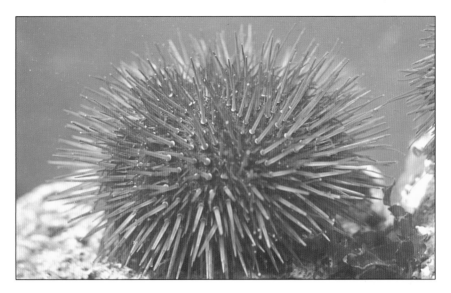

Fig. 5-11. **European Sea Urchin,** *Paracentrotus lividus* Lamarck. Inhabiting the Atlantic coasts of Europe and the Mediterranean. Diameter of the test is 6.9 centimeters (2.7 inches). From P. Giacomelli.

Fig.5-12. **White Sea Urchin,** *Tripneustes ventricosus* (Lamarck). Inhabiting the West Indies, have been incriminated. It is believed that the poison is contracted from algae upon which the sea urchins have been feeding. Diameter of the test is 7.5 centimeters (3 inches). Photograph by G. Lower.

Fig. 5-13. **Poisonous Sea Cucumber**, *Stichopus japonicus* Selenka. The tissues of this Japanese sea cucumber contain holothurin. The effects of this poison on man are unknown. Length 30.5 centimeters (12 inches). Painting by R.H. Knabenbauer.

bers is termed "holothurin" and is generally concentrated in the organs of Cuvier. Intoxications may also occur as a result of ingestion of sea cucumbers, but poisonings of this type are rare. Nothing is known concerning the symptoms produced, but fatalities have been reported.

Treatment of sea cucumber poisoning is symptomatic. There are no known antidotes.

POISONOUS ARTHROPODS

The phylum Arthropoda is the largest single group of the animal kingdom, having more than 800,000 species. Unfortunately, very little is known concerning the toxicity of most marine arthropods, the joint-legged animals which include the horseshoe crabs, lobsters, and crabs. Some of the Asiatic horseshoe crabs, tropical lobsters, and reef crabs are occasionally quite poisonous to eat.

ASIATIC HORSESHOE CRABS
FAMILY XIPHOSURIDAE

ASIATIC HORSESHOE CRAB, *Carcinoscorpius rotundicauda* (Latreille) (fig. 5-14). Poisoning from ingestion of this creature is due to eating of the unlaid green eggs or viscera during the reproductive season of the year.

Fig. 5-14. **Asiatic Horseshoe Crab**, *Carcinoscorpius rotundicauda* (Latreille). Length 33 centimeters (13 inches). Courtesy of H. Waterman.

Most of the intoxications have occurred in southeast Asia. Despite their period of toxicity, the large masses of green unlaid eggs are highly esteemed by Asiatic peoples.

Horseshoe crab poisoning, or mimi poisoning, usually occurs within thirty minutes after ingestion of the toxic eggs. Symptoms consist of dizziness; headaches; nausea; vomiting; abdominal cramps; diarrhea; cardiac palpitation; numbness of the lips; tingling of the lower extremities; weakness; loss of speech; sensation of heat in the mouth, throat, and stomach; muscular paralysis; hypersalivation; drowsiness; and loss of consciousness. The mortality rate is very high. Death may occur within sixteen hours or less.

Treatment: The treatment is symptomatic. There is no known antidote. Use the same basic procedure as in ciguatera or puffer fish poisoning.

Prevention: Although Asiatic horseshoe crabs are eaten in many parts of southeast Asia, they should be avoided during the reproductive season.

TROPICAL REEF CRABS

Although violent intoxications have been periodically reported from eating tropical reef crabs, it is only within the last few years that a serious scientific effort has been made to study the occurrence and nature of crab poisons.

There are numerous crab species that occur in tropical waters, but only a few species have been found to be toxic:

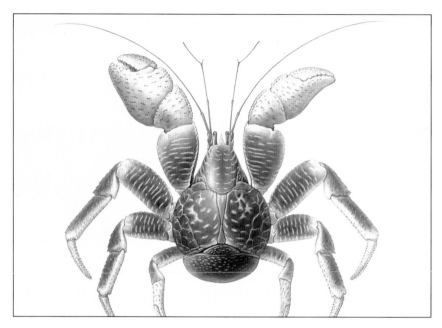

Fig. 5-15. **Coconut Crab**, *Birgus latro* (Linnaeus), which is terrestrial and found in damp jungle areas on tropical islands of the Indo-Pacific. Length of carapace is 10.7 centimeters (4.2 inches) or more. Painting by M. Shirao.

FAMILY COENOBITIDAE

COCONUT CRAB, *Birgus latro* (Linnaeus) (fig. 5-15). This toxic species is terrestrial and found in damp jungle areas on tropical islands of the Indo-Pacific. Intoxications from the coconut crab have been reported in the Ryukyu Islands. It is believed this crab becomes toxic as a result of feeding on poisonous plants. The symptoms of coconut crab poisoning include nausea, vomiting, headache, chills, fever, joint aches, exhaustion, and muscular weakness. Deaths have been reported.

Several species of tropical Indo-Pacific reef crabs have produced violent intoxications:

FAMILY ZANTHIDAE

POISONOUS REEF CRAB, *Atergatus floridus* (Linnaeus) (fig. 5-16).
RED SPOTTED CRAB, *Carpilius maculatus* (Linnaeus) (fig. 5-17).
POISONOUS REEF CRAB, *Demania toxica* Garth (fig. 5-18).
POISONOUS REEF CRAB, *Eriphia sebana* (Shaw and Nodder) (fig. 5-19).
POISONOUS REEF CRAB, *Platypodia granulosa* (Rüppell) (fig. 5-20).
POISONOUS REEF CRAB, *Zozymus aeneus* (Linnaeus) (fig. 5-21).

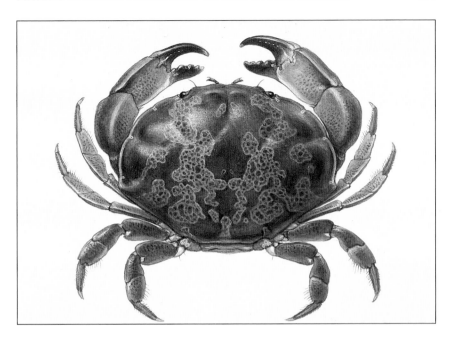

Fig. 5-16. **Reef Crab**, *Atergatus floridus* (Linnaeus). Indo-Pacific. Width of carapace is 5.1 centimeters (2 inches) or more. Painting by M. Shirao.

Fig. 5-17. **Red Spotted Crab**, *Carpilius maculatus* (Linnaeus). Indo-Pacific. Width of carapace is 13.9 centimeters (5.5 inches). W.L.R.I. photo.

Fig. 5-18. **Poisonous Reef Crab**, *Demania toxica* Garth. Indo-Pacific. Width of carapace is 43.2 millimeters (1.7 inches). Painting by R.H. Knabenbauer.

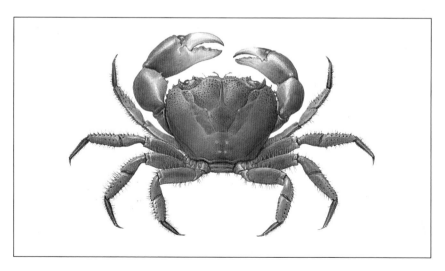

Fig. 5-19. **Poisonous Reef Crab**, *Eriphia sebana* (Shaw and Nodder). Indo-Pacific. Width of carapace is 3.3 centimeters (1.3 inches). Painting by M. Shirao.

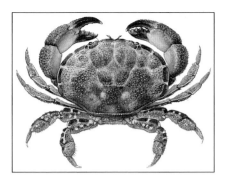

Fig. 5-20. **Poisonous Reef Crab**, *Platypodia granulosa* (Rüppell). Indo-Pacific. Painting by M. Shirao.

Medical Aspects: The symptoms produced by tropical reef crabs differ from those of the coconut crab. The symptoms include nausea, vomiting, collapse, numbness, tingling, and muscular paralysis. Death may occur in severe intoxications.

The poison is believed to be chemically identical to tetrodotoxin, the causative agent of puffer poison.

Treatment: Symptomatic, no known antidote.

Prevention: Avoid eating tropical reef crabs unless you are certain they are safe to eat. If in doubt, check with the local natives or public health authorities.

Fig. 5-21. **Poisonous Reef Crab**, *Zozymus aeneus* (Linnaeus). Tropical Indo-Pacific . Width of carapace is 5.8 centimeters (2.3 inches). Painting by M. Shirao.

Fig. 5-22. **Spiny Lobster**, *Panulirus interruptus* (Randall). Courtesy of R. Murphy, The Cousteau Society, Inc.

LOBSTERS
FAMILY PALINURIDAE

Several reports have appeared from time to time on the toxicity of lobsters found in southern Polynesia.

SPINY LOBSTER, *Panulirus interruptus* (Randall) (fig. 5-22). This specimen is a close relative of the Polynesia species.

The symptoms seem to resemble ciguatera fish poison, but little is known concerning the nature of the poison. This lobster is usually safe to eat.

CHAPTER 6

MARINE ANIMALS POISONOUS TO EAT: VERTEBRATES

POISONOUS FISHES

Tropical reef fishes may contain some of the most deadly poisons known to marine biotoxicologists. As previously indicated there are a variety of forms of ichthyosarcotoxism, or fish-flesh-poisoning. The following is a brief résumé of some of the more common types.

ELASMOBRANCH POISONING

This form of ichthyosarcotoxism is most commonly caused by eating the liver of sharks. However, the flesh of some of the larger tropical sharks and the Greenland shark, *Somniosus microcephalus,* which inhabits Arctic waters, has caused intoxications in humans and sled dogs. The chemical nature of these shark poisons is unknown. The following species have been reported to be poisonous. See also the Java Shark, on page 199.

BLACK-TIPPED REEF SHARK, *Carcharhinus melanopterus* (Quoy and Gaimard) (fig. 6-1). Indo-Pacific, South Africa to the East Indies, Hawaiian, Tuamotu, and Marianas Islands.

SEVEN-GILLED SHARK, *Heptranchias perlo* (Bonnaterre) (fig. 6-1). East and west Atlantic, Mediterranean, Cape of Good Hope, Japan.

SIX-GILLED SHARK, *Hexanchus griseus* (Bonnaterre) (fig. 6-1). Atlantic, Pacific coast of North America, Chile, Japan, Australia, Southern Indian Ocean, and South Africa.

GREENLAND SHARK, *Somniosus microcephalus* (Bloch and Schneider) (fig. 6-1). Arctic Atlantic, North Sea east to the White Sea and west to the Gulf of St. Lawrence, Greenland.

HAMMERHEAD SHARK, *Sphyrna zygaena* (Linnaeus) (See fig. 2-12 on page 30). Tropical to warm-temperate belt of the Atlantic and Pacific Oceans.

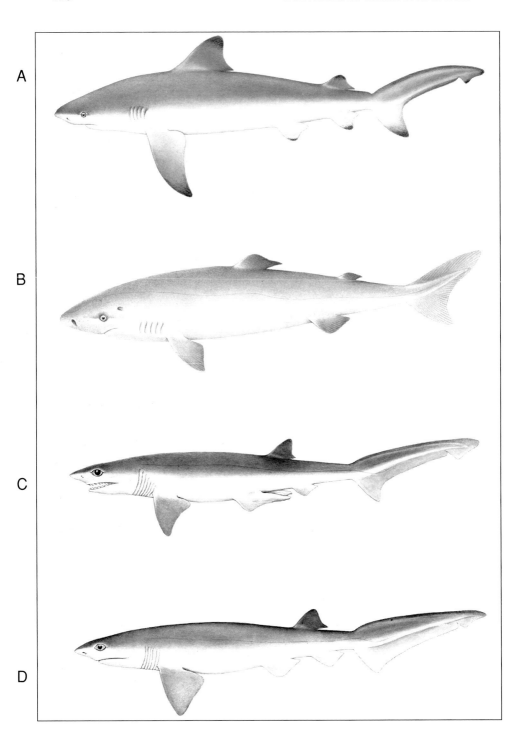

GREAT WHITE SHARK, *Carcharodon carcharias* (Linnaeus) (See fig. 2-9 on page 26). Cosmopolitan, in tropical, subtropical, and warm-temperate belts of all oceans.

Medical Aspects: The most severe forms of poisoning usually result from the eating of the liver. The musculature in most instances is only mildly toxic with the symptoms seldom more than that of a mild gastrointestinal upset and a predominating diarrhea. Symptoms from liver poisoning usually develop within thirty minutes, and consist of nausea, vomiting, diarrhea, abdominal pain, headache, joint aches, tingling about the mouth, and a burning sensation of the tongue, throat, and esophagus. As time goes on, the nervous symptoms may become progressively severe, resulting in muscular incoordination and difficulty in breathing due to muscular paralysis, coma, and finally death.

Treatment: See treatment of fish poisoning on pages 231-32.

Prevention: Avoid eating the liver of any shark unless it is known with certainty to be edible. The livers of large tropical sharks are said to be especially dangerous. The flesh of tropical and arctic sharks should be indulged in only with caution.

CIGUATERA

This is one of the most serious and widespread forms of ichthyosarcotoxism. Biotoxication is caused largely by tropical shorefishes, with more than four hundred species incriminated. Because many of the toxic species are generally regarded as valuable food, ciguatoxic fish constitute a serious threat to the development of tropical shore-fisheries. In many instances, useful food fishes suddenly, and without warning, become poisonous within a matter of hours and may remain toxic for a period of years, and it is believed that they do so because they have been feeding upon some noxious material such as algae, invertebrates, fishes, or possibly dinoflagellates. Figure 6-2 is a diagram depicting the biogenesis or transvectoring mechanism by which ciguatoxin is obtained through the food chain. There is now evidence that a dinoflagellate (*Gambierdiscus toxicus* Adachi and Fukuyo) which is frequently found on the surface of a benthic brown seaweed (*Turbinaria ornata*

◄ Fig. 6-1. *A.* **Black-Tipped Reef Shark**, *Carcharhinus melanopterus.* (Quoy and Gaimard). Length 1.9 meters (6.3 feet). *B.* **Greenland Shark**, *Somniosus microcephalus* (Bloch and Schneider). Length 1.9 meters (6.3 feet). *C.* **Seven-Gilled Shark**, *Heptranchias perlo* (Bonnaterre). Length 1.9 meters (6.3 feet). *D.* **Six-Gilled Shark**, *Hexanchus grisseus* (Bonnaterre). Length 4.7 meters (15.5 feet). The liver or flesh of these sharks may be poisonous to eat. Painting by M. Shirao.

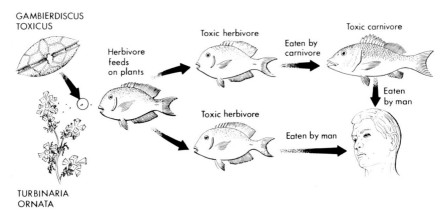

Fig. 6-2. Diagram depicting the biogenesis or transvectoring mechanism by which ciguatoxin is obtained through the food chain. Drawing By R. H. Knabenbauer.

J. Agardh) and other algae species may produce ciguatoxin. This dinoflagellate, and possibly other species as well, probably serve as the primary source of ciguatoxin. These dinoflagellates may be ingested by filter feeding invertebrates, plankton feeding fishes, herbivorous fishes feeding on marine plants, and indirectly by carnivorous fishes feeding on herbivorous fishes. It is evident that the source of ciguatoxin is due to a complex food web involvement in which a variety of environmental factors are playing a role. The food web interactions account for the widespread phylogenetic distribution of ciguatoxin among marine animals. Ciguatera is most prevalent in subtropical and tropical latitudes, but the greatest concentration of ciguatoxic fishes seems to be around the islands of the tropical Pacific, Caribbean, and Indian Oceans. Ciguatera is due to a complex of poisons, some of which are among the most deadly poisons found in marine creatures.

Until recently no good documentation on ciguatera poisoning involving sharks has been available. On November 28, 1993, in the city of Mankara, east coast of Madagascar, a single outbreak of ciguatera poisoning occurred from eating a shark, involving 500 persons, in which 98 persons died, with a case fatality rate of 20 percent. The symptomatology was typical of ciguatera. On analysis, the poison was found to differ from ciguatoxin. The shark was identified as a Java Shark, *Carcharhinus amboinensis* Müller and Henle (fig. 6-3). The shark, a female captured during the reproductive season of the year, measured 2 meters (6.5 feet) and weighed 200 kilograms (91 pounds). (Refs: *Toxicon* 32 (12): 1539-1542, 1994; *Toxin Reviews* 14 (2): 93, 1995).

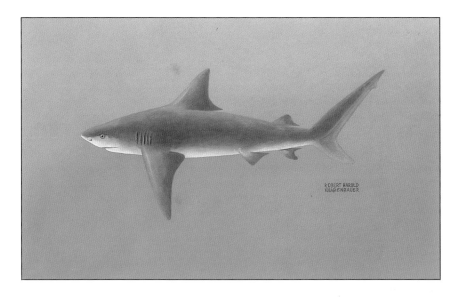

Fig. 6-3. **Java** or **Pig Eye Shark**, *Carcharhinus amboinensis* Müller & Henle. Attains a length of 2.8 meters (82 inches). The flesh of the female during the reproductive season in tropical oceans may be deadly poisonous to eat. Painting by R.H. Knabenbauer.

REPRESENTATIVE FAMILIES AND SPECIES OF CIGUATOXIC FISHES

FAMILY CARCHARHINIDAE

JAVA or PIG EYE SHARK, *Carcharhinus amboinensis* Müller and Henle (fig. 6-3). Inhabits the eastern North Atlantic, Indo-West Pacific Oceans, South Africa, Madagascar, Gulf of Aden, Indian Ocean, and Australia. This is an inshore species of the continental and insular shelves found in shallow water, near the surf, and along the beaches.

FAMILY ACANTHURIDAE—Surgeonfishes

SURGEONFISH, *Acanthurus glaucopareius* (Cuvier) (fig. 6-4). Indonesia, Philippine Islands, and tropical Pacific.

SURGEONFISH, *Acanthurus triostegus* (Linnaeus) (fig. 6-5). Tropical Indo-Pacific.

FAMILY ALBULIDAE—Bonefishes

LADYFISH, *Albula vulpes* (Linnaeus) (fig. 6-6). All warm seas.

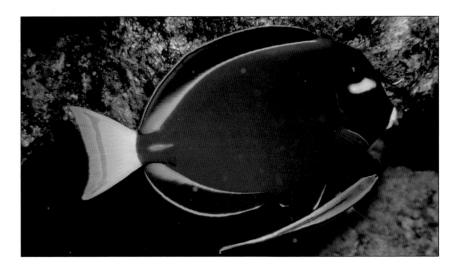

Fig. 6-4. **Surgeonfish**, *Acanthurus glaucopareius* (Cuvier). Length 30.4 centimeters (12 inches). Taken at Haputo, Guam. Courtesy of R. F. Myers.

Fig. 6-5. **Surgeonfish**, *Acanthurus triostegus* (Linnaeus). Length 25.4 centimeters (10 inches). Taken in the Red Sea. Photograph by D. Ollis.

Fig. 6-6. **Ladyfish**, *Albula vulpes* (Linnaeus). Length 1 meter (39.4 inches). Painting by S. Arita.

FAMILY ALUTERIDAE—Filefishes

FILEFISH, *Alutera scripta* (Osbeck) (fig. 6-7). All warm seas.

FAMILY BALISTIDAE—Leatherjackets

TRIGGERFISH, *Balistoides conspicillum* Bloch and Schneider (fig. 6-8). Tropical Pacific, from Polynesia to Madagascar, China, and Japan.

FAMILY CARANGIDAE—Jacks and Pompanos

JACK, *Caranx hippos* (Linnaeus) (fig. 6-9). Tropical Atlantic.
JACK, *Caranx melampygus* (Cuvier) (fig. 6-10). Tropical Pacific, north to Japan.

FAMILY HOLOCENTRIDAE—Squirrelfishes

SQUIRRELFISH, *Myripristis murdjan* (Forskål) (fig. 6-11). Indo-Pacific.

FAMILY LABRIDAE—Wrasses

WRASSE, *Coris gaimardi* (Quoy and Gaimard) (fig. 6-12). Tropical Indo-Pacific area.
WRASSE, *Epibulus insidiator* (Pallas) (fig. 6-13). Tropical Indo-Pacific.

FAMILY LUTJANIDAE—Snappers

SNAPPER, *Aprion virescens* Cuvier and Valenciennes (fig. 6-14). Tropical Indo-Pacific.

SNAPPER, *Gnathodentex aureolineatus* (Lacépède) (fig. 6-15). Tuamotu Archipelago westward to East Africa.

SNAPPER, *Lethrinus miniatus* (Forster) (fig. 6-16). Polynesia, westward to East Africa.

SNAPPER, RED, *Lutjanus bohar* (Forskål) (fig. 6-17). Tropical Pacific to east Africa and the Red Sea.

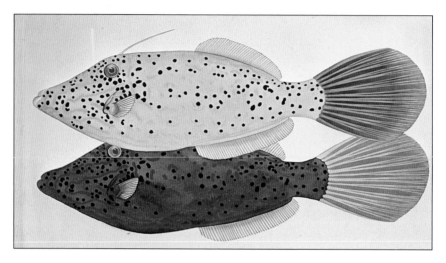

Fig. 6-7. **Filefish**, *Alutera scripta* (Osbeck). Length 50.8 centimeters (20 inches). From Hiyama.

Fig. 6-8. **Triggerfish**, *Balistoides conspicillum* Bloch and Schneider. Length 30.4 centimeters (12 inches). Painting by T. Kumada.

SNAPPER, RED, *Lutjanus gibbus* (Forskål) (fig. 6-18). Tropical Pacific to East Africa and Red Sea.

BLACK-SPOTTED SNAPPER, *Lutjanus monostigmus* (Cuvier and Valenciennes) (fig. 6-19). Polynesia, westward to the Red Sea, China.

CHINAMAN FISH, *Lutjanus nematophorus* (Bleeker) (fig. 6-20). Australia.

SNAPPER, RED, *Lutjanus vagiensis* (Quoy and Gaimard) (fig. 6-21). Polynesia, westward to East Africa, Japan.

Fig. 6-9. **Jack,** *Caranx hippos* (Linnaeus). Length 63.5 centimeters (25 inches). Painting by T. Kumada.

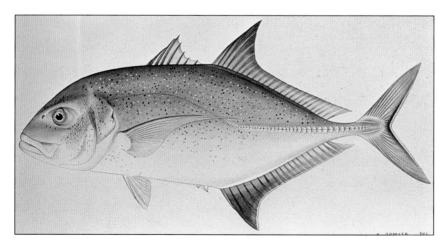

Fig. 6-10. **Jack,** *Caranx melampygus* (Cuvier). Length 63.5 centimeters (25 inches). Painting by K. Tomita.

Fig. 6-11. **Squirrelfish**, *Myripristis murdjan* (Forskål). Length 30.4 centimeters (12 inches). Courtesy of Ron Russo.

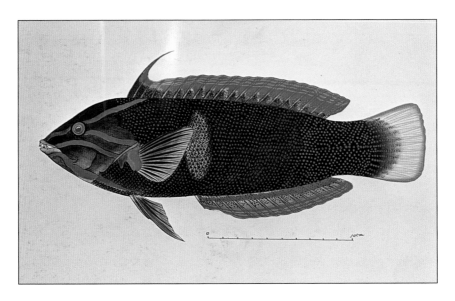

Fig. 6-12. **Wrasse**, *Coris gaimardi* (Quoy and Gaimard). Tropical Indo-Pacific area. Length 30.4 centimeters (12 inches). From Hiyama.

Fig. 6-13. **Wrasse**, *Epibulus insidiator* (Pallas). Length 30.4 centimeters (12 inches). From Hiyama.

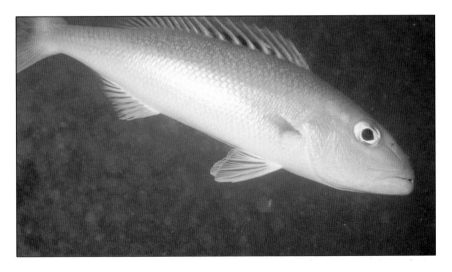

Fig. 6-14. **Snapper**, *Aprion virescens* Cuvier and Valenciennes. Length 68.5 centimeters (27 inches). Courtesy of R.F. Myers.

SNAPPER, *Monotaxis grandoculis* (Forskål) (fig. 6-22). Polynesia, westward to East Africa.

FAMILY MULLIDAE—Goatfishes

SURMULLET, GOATFISH, *Parupeneus chryserydros* (Lacépède) (fig. 6-23). Polynesia westward to East Africa.

FAMILY MURAENIDAE—Moray Eels

MORAY EEL, *Gymnothorax flavimarginatus* (Rüppell) (fig. 6-24). Tropical Indo-Pacific, coast of East Africa.

Fig. 6-15. **Snapper,** *Gnathodentex aureolineatus* (Lacépède). Length 25.4 centimeters (10 inches). Courtesy of R. F. Myers.

Fig. 6-16. **Snapper,** *Lethrinus miniatus* (Forster). Length 45.7 centimeters (18 inches). From Hiyama.

Fig. 6-17. **Snapper, Red,** *Lutjanus bohar* (Forskål). Length 88.9 centimeters (35 inches). Taken in a fish trap, Orote Cliffs, Guam. Courtesy of R.F. Myers.

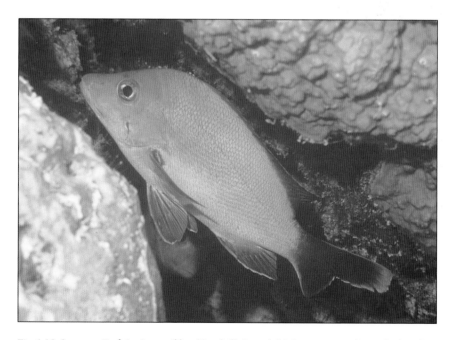

Fig. 6-18. **Snapper, Red,** *Lutjanus gibbus* (Forskål). Length 38.1 centimeters (15 inches). Taken at Palau. Courtesy of R.F. Myers.

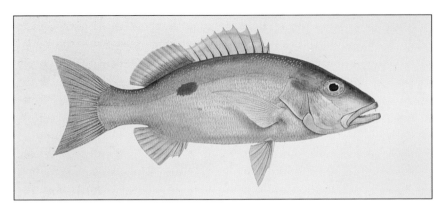

Fig. 6-19. **Black-Spotted Snapper**, *Lutjanus monostigmus* (Cuvier and Valenciennes). Length 30.4 centimeters (12 inches). From Hiyama.

Fig. 6-20. **Chinaman Fish**, *Lutjanus nematophorus* (Bleeker). Adult. Length 30.4 centimeters (12 inches). G. Coates.

MORAY EEL, *Gymnothorax javanicus* (Bleeker) (fig. 6-25). Hawaiian Islands, westward to East Africa.

MORAY EEL, *Gymnothorax meleagris* (Shaw and Nodder) (fig. 6-26). Indo-Pacific, coast of Japan.

Fig. 6-21. **Snapper, Red,** *Lutjanus vagiensis* (Quoy and Gaimard). Length 50.8 centimeters (20 inches). Painting by K. Tomita.

Fig. 6-22. **Snapper,** *Monotaxis grandoculis* (Forskål). Length 31.7 centimeters (12.5 inches). Taken at Oahu, Hawaii. Courtesy of R.F. Myers.

Fig. 6-23. **Surmullet, Goatfish,** *Parupeneus chryserydros* (Lacépède). Length 30.4 centimeters (12 inches). From Jordan and Evermann.

MORAY EEL, *Gymnothorax pictus* (Ahl) (fig. 6-27). Polynesia to East Africa. Length 75 centimeters (28 inches).

MORAY EEL, *Gymnothorax undulatus* (Lacépède) (fig. 6-28). Hawaiian Islands to the Red Sea and East Africa.

FAMILY OSTRACIIDAE—Boxfishes

SMOOTH TRUNKFISH, *Lactophrys triqueter* (Linnaeus) (fig. 6-29). Western Atlantic, tropical coasts of the Americas and Caribbean.

HORNED TRUNKFISH, *Lactoria cornuta* (Linnaeus) (fig. 6-30). Indo-Pacific, coasts of Japan, and South Africa.

FAMILY SCARIDAE—Parrotfishes

PARROTFISH, *Scarus caeruleus* (Bloch) (fig. 6-31). Florida and West Indies.

PARROTFISH, *Scarus microrhinos* Bleeker (fig. 6-32). Indo-Pacific.

FAMILY SCOMBRIDAE—Mackerels and Tunas

OCEANIC BONITO, *Euthynnus pelamis* (Linnaeus) (fig. 6-33). Circum-tropical.

FAMILY SERRANIDAE—Sea Basses

SEABASS, GROUPER, *Cephalopholis argus* Bloch and Schneider (fig. 6-34). Tropical Indo-Pacific.

SEABASS, GROUPER, *Epinephelus fuscoguttatus* (Forskål) (fig. 6-35). Indo-Pacific.

SEABASS, *Mycteroperca venenosa* (Linnaeus) (fig. 6-36). Western tropical Atlantic.

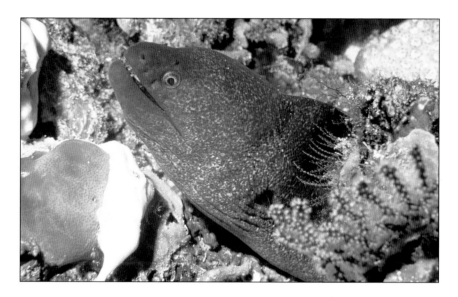

Fig. 6-24. **Moray Eel**, *Gymnothorax flavimarginatus* (Rüppell). Length 1.5 meters (5 feet). Taken at Palau. Courtesy of R.F. Myers.

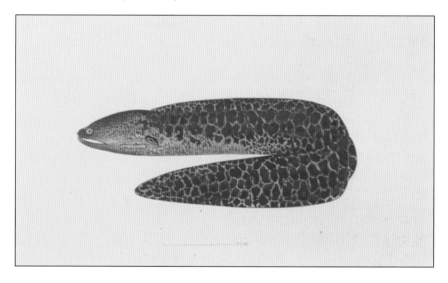

Fig. 6-25. **Moray Eel**, *Gymnothorax javanicus* (Bleeker). Length 1.5 meters (5 feet). From Hiyama.

Fig. 6-26. **Moray Eel,** *Gymnothorax meleagris* (Shaw and Nodder). Length 1 meter (39.4 inches). Taken at Palea Point, Oahu. Courtesy of R.F. Myers.

Fig. 6-27. **Moray Eel,** *Gymnothorax pictus* (Ahl). Length 71.1 centimeters (28 inches). Painting by T. Kumada.

SEABASS, *Plectropomus obligacanthus* Bleeker (fig. 6-37). Indonesia, Philippine, Caroline, and Marshall Islands.

SEABASS, *Plectropomus truncatus* (Fowler) (fig. 6-38). Micronesia, Indonesia, Philippines.

SEABASS, *Variola louti* (Forskål) (fig. 6-39). Tropical Indo-Pacific.

FAMILY SPARIDAE—Porgies

PORGIE, *Pagellus erythrinus* (Linnaeus) (fig. 6-40). Black Sea, Mediterranean, and east Atlantic, from the British Isles and Scandinavia to the Azores, Canaries, and Fernando Po.

Fig. 6-28. **Moray Eel,** *Gymnothorax undulatus* (Lacépède). Length 1.5 meters (60 inches). Taken at Guam. Photograph courtesy of R.F. Myers.

Fig. 6-29. **Smooth Trunkfish,** *Lactophrys triqueter* (Linnaeus). Length 30.4 centimeters (12 inches). W.L.R.I. photo.

FAMILY SPHYRAENIDAE—Barracudas

BARRACUDA, *Sphyraena barracuda* (Walbaum) (fig. 6-41). Indo-Pacific; from Hawaii to the Red Sea; west Atlantic from Brazil to the West Indies, Florida, and Bermuda.

FAMILY TETRAGONURIDAE—Squaretails

SQUARETAIL, *Tetragonurus cuvieri* (Risso) (fig. 6-42). Temperate regions of the world.

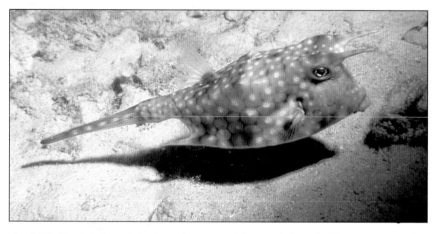

Fig. 6-30. **Horned Trunkfish,** *Lactoria cornuta* (Linnaeus). Length 30.4 centimeters (12 inches). Courtesy of R.F. Myers.

Fig. 6-31. **Parrotfish,** *Scarus caeruleus* (Bloch). Length 88.9 centimeters (35 inches). Painting by S. Arita.

Fig. 6-32. **Parrotfish**, *Scarus microrhinos* Bleeker. Length 30.4 centimeters. (12 inches). Painting by T. Kumada.

Fig. 6-33. **Oceanic Bonito**, *Euthynnus pelamis* (Linnaeus). Length 50.8 centimeters (20 inches). Painting by T. Kumada.

Medical Aspects: Symptoms of ciguatera poisoning consist of paraesthesias of the lips, tongue, and limbs, and gastrointestinal disturbances. Victims frequently complain of myalgia, joint aches, and profound muscular weakness. The so-called paradoxical sensory disturbance in which the victim interprets cold as a "tingling, burning, dry ice, or electric-shock sensation," or hot objects as cold, is characteristic of this form of poisoning. Severe neurological disturbances consisting of ataxia, generalized motor incoordi-

nation, diminished reflexes, muscular twitching, tremors, dysponia, dysphagia, clonic and tonic convulsions, coma and muscular paralysis may be
present. The case fatality rate is said to be about 12 percent. Complete
recovery may require many months, and even years in some cases.

Treatment: See pages 231-32.

CLUPEOTOXIC FISHES

Clupeotoxism is a form of ichthyosarcotoxism caused by fishes of the order
Clupeiformes, which includes the families Clupeidae, the herrings; Engraulidae, the anchovies; and other related species.

However, the families most commonly incriminated in human clupeo-
toxications are members of the Clupeidae and Engraulidae. Our knowledge
of the biotoxication is based entirely upon clinical reports scattered over a
period of several centuries.

Whether clupeotoxism is caused by a biotoxin chemically distinct from
ciguatoxin or whether the clinical evidence represents a quantitative difference in the amount of the poison ingested has not been determined. The fact
that most clupeiform fishes are largely plankton feeders and that most

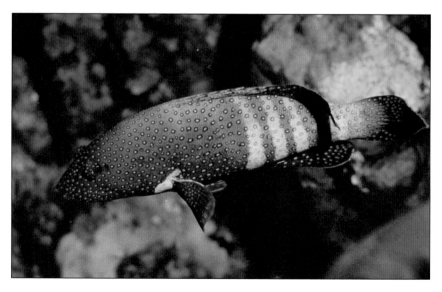

Fig. 6-34. **Seabass, Grouper,** *Cephalopholis argus* Bloch and Schneider. Length 49.5 centimeters
(19.5 inches). Courtesy of R.F. Myers.

ciguatoxic fishes are mainly bottom feeders leads one to believe that there may be a basic difference in the biotoxin involved, but at the moment this is only an assumption. Clupeotoxism is a sporadic unpredictable public health problem of the tropical Atlantic Ocean, Caribbean Sea, and the trop-

Fig. 6-35. **Seabass, Grouper,** *Epinephelus fuscoguttatus* (Forskål). Length 59.7 centimeters (23.5 inches). From Day.

Fig. 6-36. **Seabass,** *Mycteroperca venenosa* (Linnaeus). Length 88.9 centimeters (35 inches). Painting by N. Erickson.

Fig. 6-37. **Seabass,** *Plectropomus obligacanthus* Bleeker. Length 55.8 centimeters (22 inches). Painting by T. Kumada.

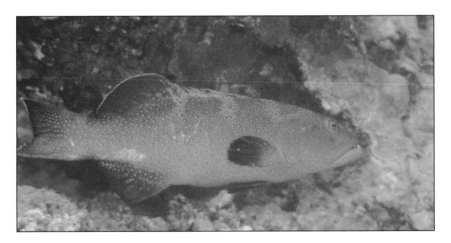

Fig. 6-38. **Seabass,** *Plectropomus truncatus* (Fowler). Length 50.8 centimeters (20 inches). Taken at Palau. Courtesy of R.F. Myers.

ical Pacific Ocean. To what extent this form of ichthyosarcotoxism occurs elsewhere is not known.

Medical Aspects: Most poisonings have occurred in the vicinity of tropical islands. Tropical clupeiform fishes are not likely to be toxic during the warm summer months. The first indication of poisoning is a sharp metallic taste which may be present immediately after ingestion of the fish. A variety of neurological symptoms may be present, and death may ensue

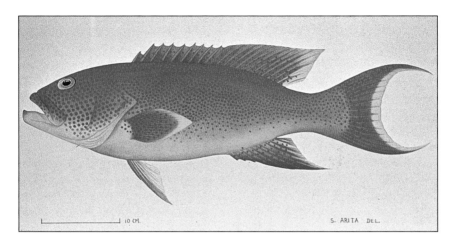

Fig. 6-39. **Seabass**, *Variola louti* (Forskål). Length 60.9 centimeters (24 inches). From Hiyama.

Fig. 6-40. **Porgie**, *Pagellus erythrinus* (Linnaeus). Length 40.6 centimeters (16 inches). From Joubin.

in less than fifteen minutes. The relationship of clupeotoxism to ciguatera fish poisoning, if any, has not been determined, since nothing is known concerning the nature of clupeotoxin.

Treatment: See pages 231-32.

REPRESENTATIVE LIST OF CLUPEOTOXIC FISHES

SPRAT, or THREAD HERRING, *Clupanodon thrissa* (Linnaeus) (fig. 6-43). Inhabits the Indo-Pacific, China, Japan, and Korea.

Fig. 6-41. **Barracuda**, *Sphyraena barracuda* (Walbaum). Length 1.5 meters (5 feet). Courtesy of P. Auerbach.

Fig. 6-42. **Squaretail**, *Tetragonurus cuvieri* (Risso). Length 25.4 centimeters (10 inches). From Goode and Bean.

ANCHOVY, *Engraulis japonicus* Schlegel (fig. 6-44). Inhabits China, Japan, Korea, and Formosa.

RED-EAR SARDINE, *Harengula humeralis* (Cuvier) (fig. 6-45). Inhabits Florida, Bermuda, and West Indies to Brazil.

SARDINE, *Harengula ovalis* (Bennett) (fig. 6-46). Inhabits the Indo-Pacific and Red Sea.

GIZZARD SHAD, *Nematolosa nasus* (Bloch) (fig. 6-47). Inhabits the Indo-Pacific, India, and Myanmar regions.

Fig. 6-43. **Sprat** or **Thread herring**, *Clupanodon thrissa* (Linnaeus). Length 25.4 centimeters (10 inches). Inhabits the Indo-Pacific, China, Japan, and Korea. From Hiyama.

Fig. 6-44. **Anchovy**, *Engraulis japonicus* Schlegel. Length 12.7 centimeters (5 inches). Inhabits China, Japan, Korea, and Formosa. Painting by S. Arita.

ANCHOVY, *Thrissina baelama* (Forskål) (fig. 6-48). Inhabits the Indo-Pacific, Red Sea, and enters river mouths.

Prevention: One cannot detect a poisonous fish by its appearance. Moreover, there is no known simple chemical test to detect the poison. The most reliable methods involve the preparation of tissue extracts which are injected intraperitoneally into mice, or feeding samples of the viscera and

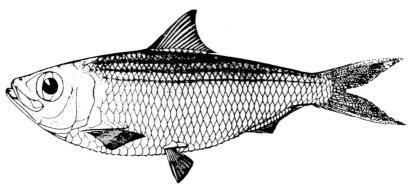

Fig. 6-45. **Red-ear sardine**, *Harengula humeralis* (Cuvier). Length 40.6 centimeters (16 inches). Inhabits Florida, Bermuda, and the West Indies to Brazil. From Rivas.

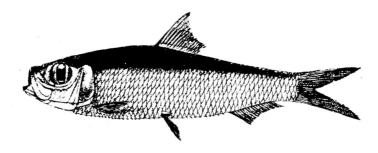

Fig. 6-46. **Sardine**, *Harengula ovalis* (Bennett). Length 15.2 centimeters (6 inches). Inhabits the Indo-Pacific and Red Sea. From Day.

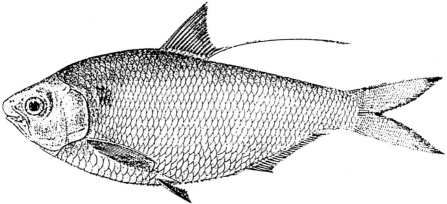

Fig. 6-47. **Gizzard shad**, *Nematolosa nasus* (Bloch). Length 20 centimeters (7.8 inches). Inhabits the Indo-Pacific, India, and Myanmar regions. From Day.

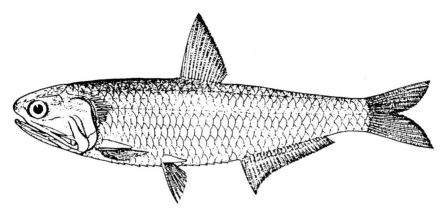

Fig. 6-48. **Anchovy,** *Thrissina baelama* (Forskål). Length 11.4 centimeters (4.5 inches). Inhabits the Indo-Pacific and Red Sea, and enters river mouths. From Daly.

flesh to laboratory animals, and observing the animal for the development of toxic symptoms. The viscera—liver and intestines—of tropical marine fishes should *never* be eaten. Also, the roe of most marine fishes is potentially dangerous, and in some cases may produce rapid death. Fishes which are unusually large for their size should be eaten with caution. This is particularly true for barracuda *(Sphyraena)*, jacks *(Caranx)*, and grouper *(Epinephelus)* during their reproductive seasons. Do not eat moray eels. Even some of the "safe" species may at times be violently poisonous.

If one is living under survival conditions, and questionable fishes must be eaten, it is advisable to cut the fish into thin fillets and to soak them in several changes of water—fresh or salt—for at least thirty minutes. Do not use the rinse water for cooking purposes. This serves to leach out the poison which is somewhat water soluble. If a questionable species is cooked by boiling, the water should always be discarded. It must be emphasized that ordinary cooking procedures do not destroy or significantly weaken the poison. The advice of native people on eating tropical marine fishes is sometimes conflicting and erroneous, particularly if they have not lived within a particular region over a period of time. Nevertheless, one should always check with the local natives as to the edibility of fish products in any tropical island area. Keep in mind that an edible fish in one region may be deadly poisonous in another region.

SCOMBROID POISONING

This form of poisoning involves the scombroid fishes which includes tuna, mackerel, skipjack, and related species. The fishes included within this category are usually edible and valuable commercial species. Scombroid poisoning is caused by improper preservation, which results in certain bacteria on the histidine in the muscle of the fish, which in turn converts the histidine to saurine, a histaminelike substance. This is the form of ichthyosarcotoxism in which bacteria play an active role in the production of the poison within the body of the fish. However, the poison is not a bacterial endotoxin.

A list of the species will not be given since any of the tuna, skipjack, bonito, mackerel, etc., may be involved. Only one species is presented here, BLUEFIN TUNA, *Thunnus thynnus* (Linnaeus) (fig. 6-49), cosmopolitan in distribution. Other representatives of these fishes are worldwide in their distribution.

Medical Aspects: Symptoms usually develop within a few minutes after ingestion of the fish. Frequently, toxic fish can be detected immediately upon tasting because of a "sharp or peppery" taste. The symptoms of scombroid poisoning resemble those of a histamine intoxication, including intense headaches, dizziness, throbbing of the large blood vessels of the neck, epigastric pain, flushing of the face, generalized erythema, urticarial eruptions, severe itching, bronchospasm, burning of the throat, cardiac palpitation, nausea, vomiting, diarrhea, abdominal pain, thirst, inability to swallow, suffocation, and severe respiratory distress. There is a danger of shock, and deaths have been reported. However, the victim usually recovers within

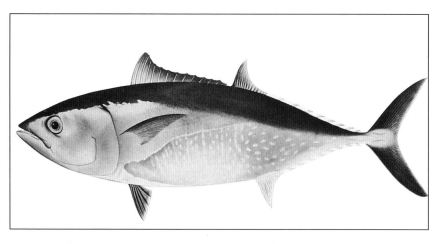

Fig. 6-49. **Bluefin Tuna,** *Thunnus thynnus* (Linnaeus). Length 2.9 meters (9.8 feet). Cosmopolitan in distribution. From Hiyama.

a period of a day or two. Scombrotoxism is believed to be the most common form of ichthyosarcotoxism on a worldwide basis.

Treatment: In addition to such routine procedures as evacuation of the stomach and catharsis, the use of any of the ordinary antihistamine drugs will be found to be effective.

Prevention: As long as properly preserved, scombroid fishes are not dangerous to eat under most circumstances. Commercially canned fish are without the slightest danger. Scombroids should be either promptly eaten soon after capture or preserved, by canning or freezing, as soon as possible. Fish left in the sun for longer than two hours should be discarded. Examine the fish before eating. If there is any evidence of staleness, such as pallor of the gills or an off-odor, discard the fish.

GEMPYLID POISONING

This form of ichthyosarcotoxism is caused by the ingestion of the flesh of fishes of the family *Gempylidae,* which includes the Castor Oil Fish, *Ruvettus pretiosus* Cocco (fig. 6-50). This fish is usually found in deep water, 400 fathoms or more, and is generally taken by hook and line at night. Although seasonal in occurrence, little is known about its habits. Ranging throughout the tropical Atlantic and Indo-Pacific Oceans, the castor oil fish is properly named because of its oily flesh and bones. Ingestion of the oil produces a diarrhea which is without cramping or other untoward effects.

No treatment is required. Many natives esteem the fish for food because of its mild purgative effect. Persons eating the fish should merely be aware of this purgative effect. The diarrhea can be stopped by not eating the fish.

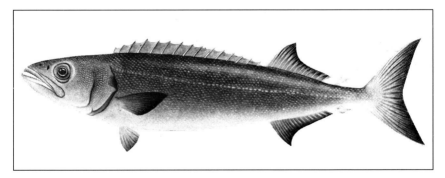

Fig. 6-50. **Castor Oil Fish,** *Ruvettus pretiosus* Cocco. Length 1.4 meters (4.1 feet). From Hiyama.

HALLUCINOGENIC FISH POISONING

A number of different species of tropical reef fishes have been known to produce hallucinations after they have been ingested. Two fishes which appear to be more commonly involved than any of the others include the Sea chub, *Kyphosus cinerascens* (Forskål) (see fig. 6-51) and the Surmullet or Goatfish, *Upeneus arge* Jordan and Evermann (see fig. 6-52). Both species are found in the Indo-Pacific region. The type of poisoning caused by ingesting these fishes is sporadic and unpredictable in its occurrence.

Medical Aspects: The poison affects primarily the central nervous system. The symptoms usually develop within a period of two hours, may persist for twenty-four hours or more, and include dizziness, loss of equilibrium, lack of motor coordination, abdominal cramps, nausea, vomiting, hallucinations, and mental depression. A tight constriction of the chest or the victim stating, "It feels like someone is sitting on my chest," are typical complaints. The victim frequently feels that he may be going to die. Actually, this is a mild form of fish poisoning, and no fatalities have been reported. Nothing is known about the nature of the poison.

Treatment: Symptomatic, but usually no treatment is required.

Prevention: Check the edibility of the fish with a local native.

PUFFER POISONING

This form of ichthyosarcotoxism is one of the most violent forms of poisoning known. It is caused by a group of fishes of the Order Tetraodontiformes, which includes puffers, porcupinefishes, and the ocean sunfishes. Puffers, which are referred to by a variety of names such as globefish, blowfish, balloonfish, toadfish, toado, swellfish, fugu, botete, fahaka, tinga, etc., are all characterized by their remarkable ability to inflate themselves by gulping in large quantities of air or water. They make considerable noise during inflation by grinding their heavy jaw teeth together. Some puffers can, and do, inflict nasty bites. Puffers have a distinctive offensive odor, which is particularly noticeable when they are dressed. Of all marine creatures puffers are among the most poisonous. The liver, gonads, intestines, and skin usually contain a powerful nerve poison, tetrodotoxin, which may produce rapid and violent death. The flesh or musculature of the fish is generally edible. Strange to say, despite the great toxicity of this fish, it commands the highest prices in Japan as food. Called fugu in Japan, puffers are prepared and sold in special restaurants where highly trained fugu cooks are used. The fugu is given careful treatment by these chefs to eliminate the danger of

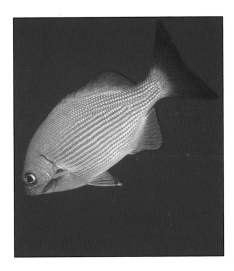

Fig. 6-51. **Sea Chub,** *Kyphosus cinerascens* (Forskål). Length 50.8 centimeters (20 inches). Taken at Guam. Courtesy of R.F. Myers.

Fig. 6-52. **Surmullet** or **Goatfish,** *Upeneus arge* Jordan and Evermann. Length 30.5 centimeters (12 inches). From Jordan and Evermann.

eating it. Nevertheless, it is still the number one cause of fatal food poisoning in Japan—especially among the lower classes, who fail to take necessary precautions. At best, eating puffer is a game of Russian roulette. Unless the services of a professional fugu chef can be obtained, it is best to leave puffers alone.

Although puffers are most numerous in the tropics, many species do extend into temperate zones (see fig. 6-53). Puffers can be recognized by their characteristic shape and large teeth.

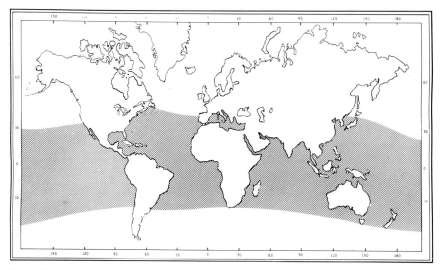

Fig. 6-53. Map showing the geographical distribution of puffers and pufferlike fishes.

The following tetradontoid fishes have been found to be poisonous:

FAMILY DIODONTIDAE

PORCUPINE FISH, *Diodon hystrix* (Linnaeus) (fig. 6-54). Circumtropical in its distribution, occasionally entering temperate areas.

FAMILY TETRADONTIDAE

PUFFER, BLOWFISH, *Arothron hispidus* (Linnaeus) (fig. 6-55).Ranges from Panama throughout the tropical Pacific, Japan to South Africa, and the Red Sea.

WHITE-SPOTTED PUFFER, *Arothron meleagris* (Lacépède) (fig. 6-56). Ranges from the west coast of Central America to Indonesia.

BLACK-SPOTTED PUFFER, *Arothron nigropunctatus* (Bloch and Schneider) (fig. 6-57). Polynesia, tropical Indo-Pacific, Japan to East Africa and the Red Sea.

GULF PUFFER, *Sphaeroides annulatus* (Jenyns) (fig. 6-58). Ranges from California to Peru and the Galapagos Islands.

Medical Aspects: Puffer poisoning is characterized by paresthesias, a tingling sensation of the lips and tongue which gradually spreads to include the extremities and later develops into severe numbness involving the entire body. Gastrointestinal disturbances may or may not be present. Respiratory

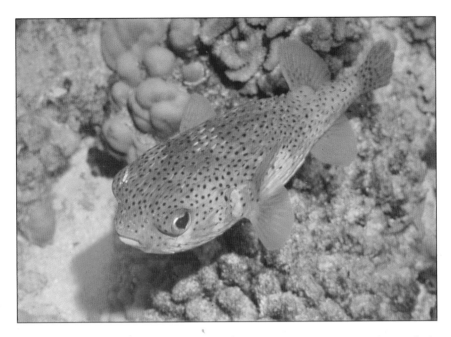

Fig. 6-54. **Porcupine Fish**, *Diodon hystrix* (Linnaeus). Length 90.2 centimeters (35.5 inches). Taken at Oahu, Hawaii. Courtesy of R.F. Myers.

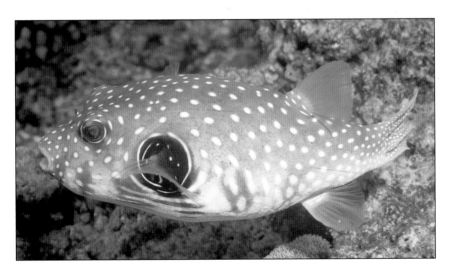

Fig. 6-55. **Puffer, Blowfish,** *Arothron hispidus* (Linnaeus). Length 53.3 centimeters (21 inches). Taken at Waikiki Aquarium, Hawaii. Courtesy of R.F. Myers.

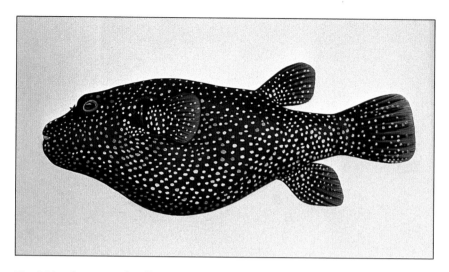

Fig. 6-56. **White-Spotted Puffer**, *Arothron meleagris* (Lacépède). Length 33 centimeters (13 inches). Painting by S. Arita.

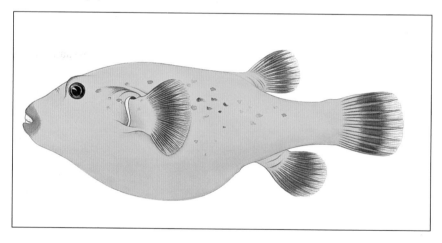

Fig. 6-57. **Black-Spotted Puffer**, *Arothron nigropunctatus* (Bloch and Schneider). Length 25.9 centimeters (10 inches). Painting by S. Arita.

distress is a prominent part of the clinical picture, and the victim eventually becomes intensely cyanotic. Petechial hemorrhages, blistering, and severe scaling of the skin may develop. Ataxia, aphonia, dysphagia, muscular twitchings, tremors, incoordination, paralysis, and convulsions are frequently present. The victim may become comatose, but in most instances remains conscious until shortly before death. Treatment is symptomatic.

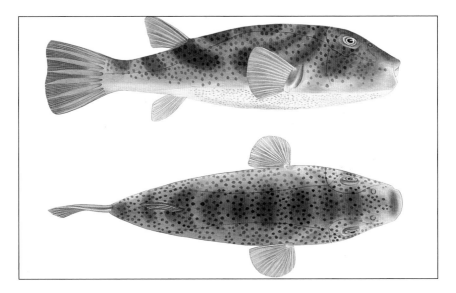

Fig. 6-58. **Gulf Puffer**, *Sphaeroides annulatus* (Jenyns). Length 25.9 centimeters (10 inches). Painting by T. Kumada.

The case fatality rate is about 60 percent. If death occurs, it usually takes place within the first twenty-four hours.

Pharmacological studies have shown that the primary action of tetrodotoxin is on the nervous system, producing both central and peripheral effects. Relatively low doses of the poison will readily inhibit neuromuscular function. Major effects include respiratory failure and hypotension. It is believed that puffer fish poison has a direct action on respiratory centers; there is also some evidence that tetrodotoxin depresses the vasomotor center.

Treatment: See treatment of fish poisoning. There is no specific treatment or antidote for puffer poisoning.

Prevention: Learn to recognize the puffer and leave it alone.

GENERAL TREATMENT FOR FISH POISONING

With the exception of scombroid poisoning, in which the patient should be administered antihistaminic drugs, there is no specific treatment. However, a few general procedures have been of value in many instances.

The stomach should be emptied at the earliest possible moment. Warm salt water, or egg white, will be found effective. If these ingredients are not available, stick a finger down the throat. A cathartic should be administered. In many instances 10 percent calcium gluconate given intravenously has given prompt relief from some of the nervous symptoms, whereas in others it has not. Paraldehyde and ether inhalations have been reported to be effective in controlling the convulsions. Nikethamide or one of the other respiratory stimulants is advisable in cases of respiratory depression. In patients where excessive production of mucus is present, aspiration and constant turning are essential. Atropine has been found to make the mucus more viscid and difficult to aspirate and is not recommended. If laryngeal spasm is present, intubation and tracheotomy may be necessary. Oxygen inhalation and intravenous administration of fluids supplemented with vitamins given parenterally are usually beneficial. If the pain is severe, opiates will be required. Morphine is the drug of choice when given in small, divided doses. Cool showers have been found to be effective in relieving the severe itching. It should be kept in mind that in rare instances scombroid poisoning may be combined with other types of fish poisoning. Fluids given to patients suffering from disturbances of temperature sensation should be slightly warm, or at room temperature. Vitamin B complex supplements are advisable.

POISONOUS MARINE TURTLES

Poisoning from marine turtles is one of the lesser known types of intoxications produced by marine organisms. The cases that have been reported are sufficiently severe to be impressive. As in the case of fishes, most of these species are commonly eaten with impunity. For some unknown reason, certain species of marine turtles in the vicinity of the Philippine Islands, Sri Lanka, and Indonesia, under certain circumstances, may become extremely poisonous to eat.

SPECIES OF MARINE TURTLES REPORTED AS POISONOUS TO EAT

FAMILY CHELONIDAE

GREEN SEA TURTLE, *Chelonia mydas* (Linnaeus) (fig. 6-59). Inhabits all tropical and subtropical oceans.

HAWKSBILL TURTLE, *Eretomochelys imbricata* (Linnaeus) (fig. 6-60). Inhabits all tropical and subtropical seas.

FAMILY DERMOCHELIDAE

LEATHERBACK TURTLE, *Dermochelys coriacea* (Linnaeus) (fig. 6-61). Largely circumtropical but occasionally taken in temperate waters.

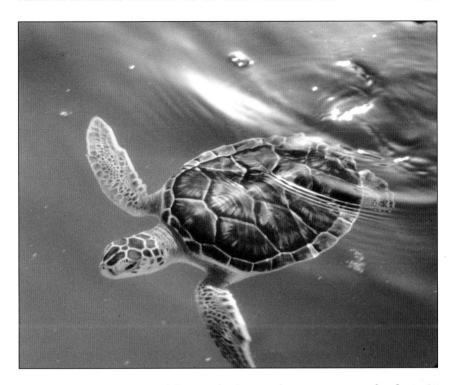

Fig. 6-59. **Green Sea Turtle**, *Chelonia mydas* (Linnaeus). May attain a weight of over 25 kilograms (55 pounds) and a carapace length of about 1.2 meters (4 feet). Taken at Heron Island, Australia. Courtesy of D. Perrine.

Medical Aspects: Symptoms generally develop within a few hours to several days after ingestion of the flesh. The initial symptoms are usually nausea, vomiting, diarrhea, severe upper abdominal pain, dizziness, dry burning sensation of the lips, tongue, lining of the mouth and throat. Swallowing becomes very difficult, and excessive salivation is pronounced. The disturbances of the mouth may take several days to develop but become progressively severe as time goes on. The breath becomes very foul. The tongue develops a white coating and may become covered with multiple pinhead-sized, reddened papules which may later break down into ulcers. If the victim has been severely poisoned, he tends to become very sleepy and is difficult to keep awake. If this symptom develops, it is usually a bad sign as death soon follows. About 44 percent of the victims poisoned by marine turtles die. Death is believed to be due to liver and kidney damage.

Treatment: There is no specific treatment. Some of the recommendations presented in fish poisoning are pertinent here.

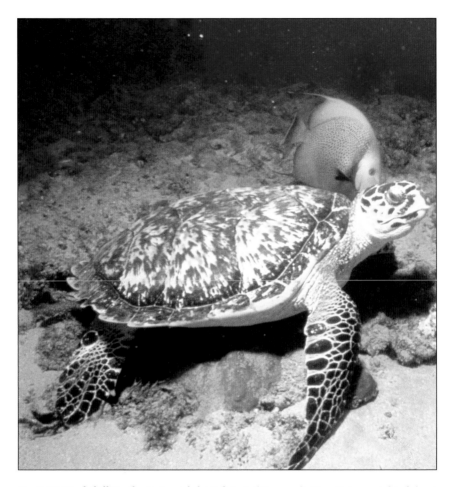

Fig. 6-60. **Hawksbill Turtle**, *Eretomochelys imbricata* (Linnaeus). May attain a weight of about 124.9 kilograms (275 pounds) and a carapace length of about 85.1 centimeters (33.5 inches). Courtesy of D. Perrine.

Prevention: Marine turtles in the tropical Indo-Pacific region should be eaten with caution. If in doubt, a check with local native groups will determine if they are safe to eat in that locality. Turtle liver is especially dangerous to eat.

MARINE MAMMALS

Several species of marine mammals have been incriminated in human intoxications. These include:

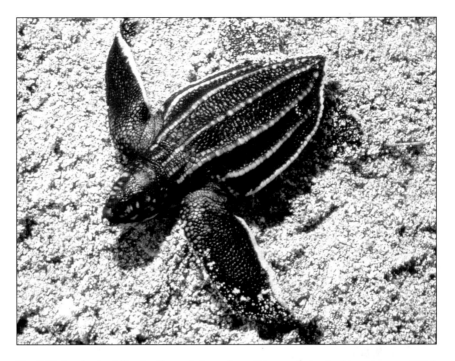

Fig. 6-61. **Leatherback Turtle**, *Dermochelys coriacea* (Linnaeus). Attains large size, over 250.2 kilograms (551 pounds) and a carapace length of about 1.2 meters (4 feet). Courtesy of D. Perrine.

FAMILY PHOCIDAE

BEARDED SEAL, *Erignathus barbatus* (Erxleben) (fig. 6-62). This species is circumboreal in its distribution, living at the edge of ice. Its liver is said to contain a high concentration of vitamin A, and may be as toxic as polar bear liver.

AUSTRALIAN SEA LION, *Neophoca cinerea* (Peron) (fig. 6-63). This sea lion is confined to the coast of South Australia. The flesh of this animal is said to be toxic, but there is very little supporting data upon which to base any conclusions.

FAMILY URSIDAE

POLAR BEAR, *Thalarctos maritimus* Phipps (fig. 6-64). Ranges throughout the Arctic regions of the world. Numerous poisonings have resulted from eating the liver and kidneys of polar bears. The predominant symptoms are intense throbbing or dull frontal headaches, nausea, severe scaling of

Fig. 6-62. **Bearded Seal**, *Erignathus barbatus* (Erxleben). Length 2.7 meters (9 feet). Painting by R.H. Knabenbauer.

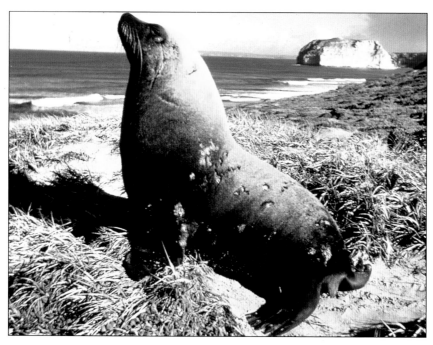

Fig. 6-63. **Australian Sea Lion**, *Neophoca cinerea* (Peron). Length 2.4 meters (8 feet). Courtesy of B.J. Marlow.

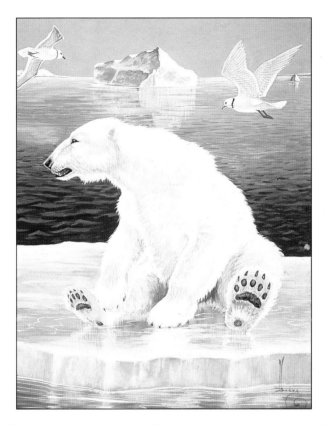

Fig. 6-64. **Polar Bear**, *Thalarctos maritimus* Phipps. Attains a length of 2.4 meters (8 feet) and a weight of 681 kilograms (1500 pounds). Ingestion of the liver and kidneys of the polar bear may result in a fatal intoxication due to hypervitaminosis A. Illustration by H. Baerg.

the skin, vomiting, diarrhea, abdominal pain, dizziness, drowsiness, irritability, collapse, photophobia, and convulsions. Fatalities are rare. Polar bear poisoning consists of central nervous system manifestations primarily due to an abrupt and marked elevation of spinal fluid pressure.

Polar bear poisoning is believed to be related to an excessive intake of Vitamin A, which is known to be present in the liver and kidneys of these bears. Symptoms develop in adults with the ingestion of about one million international units of Vitamin A. Seven million international units may be fatal.

It has been suggested that other toxic substances in addition to Vitamin A may also be present, but this has not been determined with any degree of certainty.

Fig. 6-65 *Left*, **Sei Whale**, *Balaenoptera borealis* Lesson. Length 18 meters (59 feet). *Right*, **Sperm Whale**, *Physeter catodon* Linnaeus. Length 18 meters (59 feet). Painting by R.H. Knabenbauer.

WHALES AND PORPOISES

Several species of marine mammals have been reported as having poisonous flesh or viscera. The species incriminated are as follows:

FIN BACK WHALES: FAMILY BALAENOPTERIDAE

SEI WHALE, *Balaenoptera borealis* Lesson (fig. 6-65, *left*). Intoxications have been reported from eating the liver of this whale. Symptoms consist of severe occipital headaches; neck pain; flushing and swelling of the face; nausea; vomiting; diarrhea; fever; chills; photophobia; an abnormal flow of tears; erratic blood pressure; dryness of the lips; and desquamation around the mouth, cheeks, and forehead. Acute symptoms gradually subside within about two days. Ranges from the coast of Labrador, southward to Campeche,

Mexico, in the Atlantic Ocean; Bering Sea, southward to Baja California, in the Pacific Ocean.

SPERM WHALE: FAMILY PHYSETERIDAE

SPERM WHALE, *Physeter catodon* Linnaeus (fig. 6-65, *right*). The oil and flesh have been reported as toxic. The symptomatology is not known. Inhabits polar, temperate, and tropical seas.

WHITE WHALE: FAMILY MONODONTIDAE

WHITE WHALE or BELUGA, *Delphinapterus leucas* (Pallas) (fig. 6-66, *bottom*). Ingestion of the flesh has been reported to cause fatalities. Inhabits Arctic seas, but may ascend rivers.

Fig. 6-66 *Top,* **Southeast Asiatic Porpoise**, *Neophocaena phocaenoides* (Cuvier). Length 1.5 meters (5 feet). *Bottom,* **White whale** or Be-**luga**, *Delphinapterus leucas* (Pallas). Length 5.5 meters (18 feet). Painting by R.H. Knabenbauer.

PORPOISES: FAMILY DELPHENIDAE

SOUTHEAST ASIATIC PORPOISE, *Neophocaena phocaenoides* (Cuvier) (fig. 6-66, *top*). Ingestion of the liver and other viscera have been reported as toxic, causing abdominal pain, nausea, abdominal swelling, numbness of the tongue, loss of vision, cyanosis, numbness of various areas of the skin, hypersalivation (with a greenish tinge to the saliva), and muscular paralysis. Fatalities may occur. Inhabits the coastal areas of China, Japan, Sumatra, and India to South Africa, and may enter rivers and estuaries.

Treatment: Emetics and laxatives promptly administered are sometimes useful in relieving symptoms. The clinical symptoms gradually disappear after ingestion of the toxic material has been discontinued.

Prevention: There is no reliable method of detecting toxic marine mammal poisons by mere visual examination. The age of the animal has no bearing on its edibility; young animals may cause poisoning as well as older ones.

CHAPTER 7

OTHER DANGEROUS
AQUATIC ANIMALS

Electric fishes are small in number, but constitute a fascinating assemblage of dangerous aquatic animals. Although most plants and animals produce electrical discharges of some type, there are only about 250 species of fishes known to possess actual specialized electric organs. However, many other species of fishes are known to emit electrical discharges through their lateral line system.

Electricity is an important constituent in the metabolic activity of living things. The amount of current is so small in many instances that these currents can be detected only by extremely sensitive instruments. In land animals, the air acts as a good insulator, and these small discharges are very difficult to detect at any distance from the body. With animals living in an aquatic medium, the water acts as a good conductor, and some aquatic animals possess a specialized organ system that discharges electricity through the water at surprisingly high voltages.

The best known and most studied of the electric aquatic organisms are described below.

ELECTRIC AQUATIC ANIMALS

ELECTRIC EELS: FAMILY ELECTROPHORIDAE

There is only a single species in this family:

ELECTRIC EEL, *Electrophorus electricus* (Linnaeus) (fig. 7-1). This eel inhabits the streams and swamps of South American jungles, and is the most powerful of the electric fishes. An air breather, it must periodically surface for a gulp of air, or it will drown. This eel is able to produce an enormous amount of electricity—up to about 650 volts, with an average 40 watts—sufficient to light up an electric bulb. When this current is discharged into the water, the electrical field that it sets up is sufficient to stun a man or even a horse.

Fig. 7-1. **Electric Eel**, *Electrophorus electricus* (Linnaeus). Attains a length of 1.2 meters (4 feet) or more. Courtesy of G. Ruggieri, New York Aquarium.

When at rest, *Electrophorus* gives off no electricity, but when swimming it will emit a discharge of about 50 volts at a rate of about 50 per second. Since this eel develops cataracts at an early age, possibly due to the electrical discharges, the electrolocation system is of considerable importance to its survival. Although the discharge lasts only two one-thousandths of a second, the eel can send out 400 or more per second. An eel can give out a steady series of discharges for twenty minutes, rest for five minutes, and then continue the shocking process again. It is truly one of the world's most efficient batteries.

Another well known group of electric fishes are the marine torpedo rays, which include species that are the second most potent dischargers of electricity. Large torpedo rays can give off more than 200 volts. Representative species include:

TORPEDO RAYS: FAMILY NARCINIDAE

LESSER ELECTRIC RAY, *Narcine brasiliensis* (Olfers) (fig. 7-2), is found in the inshore waters of the western Atlantic, from Brazil to Florida and Texas, south to Argentina.

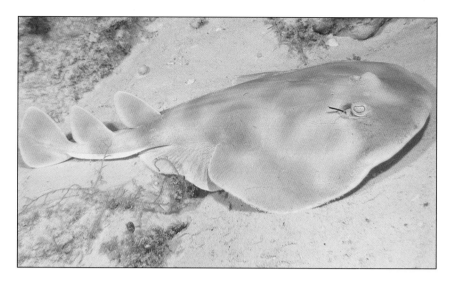

Fig. 7-2. **Lesser Electric Ray,** *Narcine brasiliensis* (Olfers). Length 42 centimeters (11 inches). Is found in the inshore waters of the western Atlantic, from Brazil to Florida and Texas, south to Argentina. Courtesy of D. Gotshall.

BULL'S EYE TORPEDO or ELECTRIC RAY, *Diplobatis omata* (Jordan and Gilbert) (fig. 7-3), which ranges in the inshore waters of the southern California coast.

MARBLED CRAMPFISH or TORPEDO RAY, *Torpedo marmorata* Risso (fig. 7-4), which also inhabits the Mediterranean Sea.

The electric rays are sluggish, feeble swimmers that spend most of their time lying on the bottom partially buried in the mud or sand at shallow depths.

The Greeks knew the torpedo rays and referred to them as the "narke," a term from which the words narcotic and narcosis are derived. Many Roman physicians used these torpedo rays to shock their patients. Thus, electrotherapy is a very ancient modality.

There are numerous other electric fishes that are not as well known as the electric eels and torpedoes. One of these is:

ELECTRIC CATFISHES: FAMILY MALAPTERURIDAE

ELECTRIC CATFISH, *Malapterurus electricus* Lacépède (fig. 7-5). This electric catfish inhabits a wide range of streams and rivers of Africa, extending from the Nile to the Zambezi rivers, but is absent from most of the rivers of East Africa. Electric catfishes are also sluggish creatures, spending much

Fig. 7-3. **Bull's Eye Torpedo** or **Electric Ray**, *Diplobatis omata* (Jordan and Gilbert). Length 60.9 centimeters (2 feet). Courtesy of D. Gotshall.

Fig. 7-4. **Marbled Crampfish** or **Torpedo Ray**, *Torpedo marmorata* Risso. Length 70 centimeters (27.3 inches). Courtesy of P. Giacomelli.

Fig. 7-5. **Electric Catfish**, *Malapterurus electricus* Lacépède. Length 61.9 centimeters (2 feet). Painting by R.H. Knabenbauer.

of their time on the bottom in the mud. Larger specimens of *Malapterurus* are said to produce a discharge of up to 450 volts. They have been observed in an aquarium shocking other fishes, causing them to vomit up their meals, which are quickly ingested by *Malopterurus*. Certainly this is one of the world's most unique methods of procuring food. Normally they feed chiefly on decomposing vegetable and animal matter.

Electric catfish were well known to ancient Egyptians and were depicted on the murals and tombs of Ti at Sakkara and in the great fishing scene at Giza. The electric catfish, which was referred to as the "torpedo," was also known to ancient Abyssinians and was noted as follows in the book *Abassia*, viz.: "In thefe Rivers and Lakes is alfo found the Torpedo, which if any man hold in his hand, if it ftirse not, it doth produce no effect, but if it mouv it felfe never fo little, it fo tormenth the body of him which holds it, that his Arteries, Joints, Sinews, & all his numbers feele exceeding paine. . . ." (*See* Wu, 1984.)

Because of its unique electrical properties, *Malapterurus* was used for its medicinal properties by physicians of ancient Middle Eastern countries. The shocking process by electric fishes was used in ancient times for the treatment of rheumatism. The Arab physician Ibn-Sidah claimed that a live electric catfish placed on the brow of an epileptic victim was beneficial. It is significant that in World War II, the electric organs of the electric eel, *Electro-*

phorus, were used as a potential antiwar gas agent. Maybe the ancient "witch doctors" were ahead of their time.

Another interesting group of electric fishes includes the following:

STARGAZERS: FAMILY URANOSCOPIDAE

SOUTHERN STARGAZER, *Astroscopus y-graecum* (Cuvier and Valenciennes) (fig. 7-6), which inhabits the south Atlantic coast from Cape Hatteras to the Caribbean Sea, has been studied to only a limited extent. The electrogenic organs of stargazers are located in a specialized pouch just behind the eyes. The uranoscopids are also equipped with venomous shoulder spines. Their electrogenic organs are said to be modified eye muscles. When at rest, *Astroscopus* discharges only about 90 millivolts, but is capable of releasing up to 50 volts when necessary.

Fig. 7-6. **Southern Stargazer,** *Astroscopus y-graecum* (Cuvier and Valenciennes). Length 38.1 centimeters (15 inches). Courtesy of Miami Seaquarium.

Some of the electric fishes are quite bizarre in their appearance. The elephantfishes of the family Mormyridae have an oddly-shaped mouth that is extremely variable in appearance. In some species, there is a very elongate proboscis-like snout with a terminal mouth. An example of the *Mormyrus* species is:

ELEPHANTFISHES: FAMILY MORMYRIDAE

ELEPHANTNOSE or SNOUTFISH, *Mormyrus tapirus* Pappenheim (fig. 7-7), which is known to produce low voltage discharges at a rather steady rate. Mormyrids have poor eyesight and live in the murky water in the Nile River and tropical Africa. They set up an electrical field around them so that

Fig. 7-7. **Elephantnose** or **Snoutfish**, *Mormyrus tapirus* Pappenheim. Length 28 centimeters (11 inches). Painting by R.H. Knabenbauer.

when anything breaks this field, they are readily able to detect the object. The mormyrids are closely related to another species of electric fish:

UBANGI MORMYRID, *Gnathonemus petersi* (Günther) (fig. 7-8), which also discharges low voltage electricity.

Another species producing an electrical discharge is:

FAMILY GYMNARCHIDAE

JERFAR, *Gymnarchus niloticus* Cuvier (fig. 7-9), which is the only species in the family Gymnarchidae. Laboratory studies have shown that this fish can distinguish between objects having identical geometric and optical properties but having different conductivities. The Mormyrids and *Gymnarchus* appear to have small specialized electrical organs located in the posterior part of their bodies.

NAKED-BACK KNIFEFISHES: FAMILY GYMNOTIDAE

CARAPO, *Gymnotus carapo* Linnaeus (fig. 7-10), a member of the family Gymnotidae, or naked-back knifefish, is an air breather like *Electrophorus*. It inhabits the freshwaters of Central and South America. The carapo discharges electricity as a continuous series of low-intensity impulses at the rate of 65 per second.

Fig. 7-8. **Ubangi Mormyrid**, *Gnathonemus petersi* (Günther). This fish has a unique look, with the lower jaw cylindrical, having a tapering dermal appendage, giving the fish a "Ubangi" appearance. The Mormyrids usually discharge only a low-voltage electricity. These fish have poor eyesight and live in murky water. Most of their food detection and avoidance of enemies is by means of electrolocation. They inhabit the waters of central Africa. Length 22.8 centimeters (9 inches) or more. Taken at the New York Aquarium. Courtesy of G. D. Ruggieri, New York Aquarium, New York Zoological Society.

Fig. 7-9. **Jerfar**, *Gymnarchus niloticus* Cuvier. Length 1 meter (39 inches). From Boulenger.

Fig. 7-10. **Carapo**, *Gymnotus carapo* Linnaeus. Length 38.1 centimeters (15 inches). After Axelrod and Schultz. Painting by R. H. Knabenbauer.

Members of the knifefish family Rhamphichthyidae of the freshwater streams of South America also possess electrogenic organs.

Numerous other fishes also possess specialized electric organs. The following is a partial list of fish genera known to have electric organs: The elephantfishes, *Genyomyrus*, *Gnathoneumus*, *Hyperopisus*, *Marcusenius*, *Mormyrops*, *Mormyrus*, *Petrocephalus*; the knifefish *Hypopomus*; glass knifefish, *Eigenmania*; naked knifefish, *Adontosternarchus*, *Sternarchus*; and the electric rays, *Raja*.

ELECTRIC ORGANS OF FISHES

The electric organs of fishes are said to be derived from muscle or nerve tissue. Although a few fish, such as the electric eel, *Electrophorus*, can produce potent discharges of up to 650 volts, most electric fishes emit discharges in the range of millivolts up to several volts. Strong discharges are emitted infrequently and are used to deter as a defense mechanism or to stun their prey. Weak discharges are emitted continuously and are used as a system of electrolocation and social communication.

The answer to the question as to how fishes generate electricity has intrigued scientists for many years and has stimulated an enormous amount of research. The electric organs of fishes are believed to function on the following principles:

Specialized electrocytes (electric cells) that are arranged in series are synchronously excited by spinal nerve signals to generate small voltage gradients in the direction of their linear arrangement. Since each stack of electrocytes is tightly surrounded by insulating tissues, the voltage contributions of the electrocytes add linearly, as with a series of small batteries. Figure 7-11 shows the general anatomical structure of the electric eel.

The electric ray is arranged differently (fig. 7-12). Here, the electric organs constitute about one-sixth of the total body weight and are situated one on either side of the anterior part of the disc between the anterior extension of the pectoral fin and the head, and extend from about the level of the eye backward past the gill region.

The process of electrolocation (fig. 7-13) resembles echo or sonar location in the sense that the animal assesses its environment by actively emitting signals and monitoring their feedback. One of the benefits of the systems used by electro- and echolocating animals is that they can operate effectively in total darkness. The fish generates a current field that emanates from its anterior body and then converges on the tip of its tail (fig. 7-14).

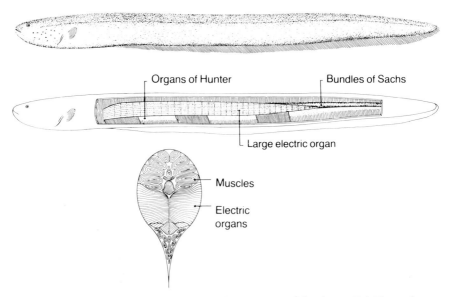

Fig. 7-11. Illustration of the general anatomical arrangement of the **Electric Eel**, *Electrophorus electricus*. There are three separate electric organs. The *large electric organ* is the main battery. This is the electric organ from which the large discharges are released. This organ is paired, one on either side of the tail of the fish. It starts just behind the body of the fish and continues to a point about two-thirds down the tail. At this point, the large electric organ diminishes in size and is replaced by two smaller paired electric organs known as the *bundles of Sachs*. The arrangement of cells is similar in both organs, but the cells of the bundles of Sachs are larger. There is a third set of electric organs known as the *organs of Hunter*. They are very slender, extending throughout the entire length of the anal fin along the base of the fin. The discharge of the organs of Hunter appears to be influenced by the large electric organ. The electric cells that fill the organs are arranged in series-parallel in the fish, but prevail in series. Their voltage is about 0.1 volt. They vary in size dependent upon the size of the fish. The polarity in the eel is positive at the head and negative at the tail. There is no reversal of polarity. Drawing by R. Kreuzinger, after Coates.

Electroreceptors distributed over the anterior body surface monitor local current flowing over the skin produced by the electric organ discharge. The electroreceptors are derived from the lateral line organs and are supplied by lateral line nerves. It is interesting to note that the lateral line system is composed of sensory cells that resemble hair cells of the inner ear of humans. An object that differs in impedance (opposition in an electrical circuit) from the surrounding water distorts the electric field and thereby alters the pattern of electrical current intensities over the body of the fish that is closest to the object. Thus, by monitoring local changes in electroreceptor activity, the fish

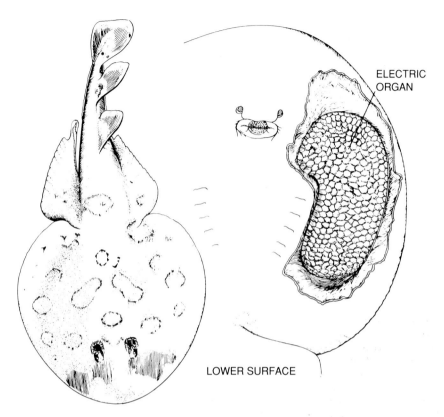

Fig. 7-12. **Lesser electric ray**, *Narcine braciliensis* (Olfers) with the skin removed to show the arrangement of the electric organs. Contact with the skin can result in a severe electric shock long to be remembered. It can discharge up to 200 volts. The polarity of the electric organ is positive on the dorsal side and negative on the underside. This fish inhabits the western Atlantic from Brazil to Florida and Texas, south to Argentina. Length 27.9 centimeters (11 inches). After Bigelow and Schroeder.

is able to perceive the presence and nature of objects. Electric fishes are truly one of the marvels of the aquatic world and offer a wealth of material for future research into the phenomena of electrolocation.

HUMAN PARASITIC CATFISH

Although the human parasitic catfish are freshwater, because their medical significance is of such an unusual nature, they have been added to this book.

Stories concerning catfishes that penetrate the human urethra have issued from the Amazon jungle for centuries. It is now known that these

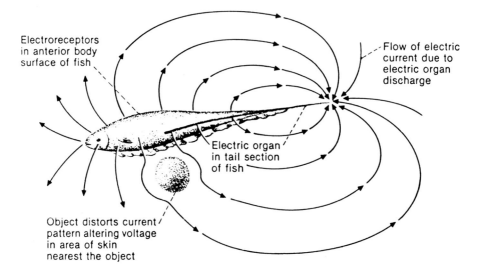

Electroreceptors
in anterior body
surface of fish

Flow of electric
current due to
electric organ
discharge

Electric organ
in tail section
of fish

Object distorts current
pattern altering voltage
in area of skin
nearest the object

Fig. 7-13. Diagram showing the principles of electrolocation. The longitudinal black bar in the tail of the fish indicates the location of the electric organ. The electroceptors are situated in a series of pores on the anterior body surface of the fish. Drawing by R. H. Knabenbauer.

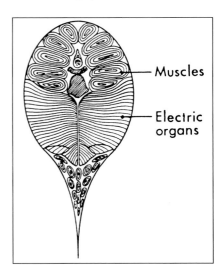

Muscles

Electric
organs

Fig. 7-14. Cross section of the tail of the electric eel, showing the anatomical relationship of electric organs to muscle mass. Drawing by R. Kreuzinger, after Coates.

Fig. 7-15. Photograph of *Urinophilus erythrurus* Eigenmann. Because of its shape and small size, this catfish is capable of invading the urethra and other orifices of the body. Attains a length of up to 20.3 centimeters (8 inches). J. Tashijan.

catfishes are members of the family *Pygidiidae,* and one genus has been appropriately designated as *Urinophilus,* or a "lover of urine." Natives refer to these fish as the "candirú" or "canero." Documented reports have cited instances in which the candirú is known to have penetrated the urethra, vagina, and rectum of humans and other animals. Most of the candirú capable of urinary misconduct are either juvenile or small specimens. They are generally elongated or eellike in form (fig. 7-15), cylindrical to tetrate in cross section, have a rounded depressed head, and an inferiorly placed mouth. The body of these fishes are scaleless, slimy, having a transparent or flesh to brownish color. The dangerous candirú are about 3 to 50 millimeters ($\frac{1}{8}$–2 inches) in length. The candirú is a formidable parasite to have clinging to one's urethra because of its fanglike erectile teeth in front of the mouth, and the opercular spines situated on either gill cover, and on the head (fig. 7-16). Natives wading in streams inhabited by the candirú wear a variety of protective devices hoping to barricade any intrusion by these devilish beasts (fig. 7-17).

Once the candirú invades the urethra, vagina, or rectum they usually have to be surgically removed.

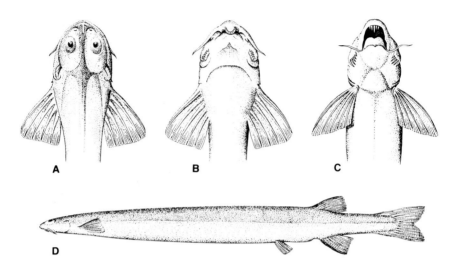

Fig. 7-16. Drawing of the parasitic candirú catfish of the Amazon. *A.* Dorsal view of head of *Urinophilus. B.* Ventral view of the head, showing opercular spines of the head. *C.* Ventral view of the head of *Vandellia cirrhosa* Cuvier and Valenciennes, a related candirú species. Note the teeth of the upper jaw and gill covers. These are the spines which prevent the catfish from being removed once the fish has penetrated the body. *D.* Side view of *U. erythrurus.* Drawing by R. Kreuzinger, after Gudger.

SCHISTOSOMAL DERMATITIS

This is a type of dermatitis due to the penetration of the skin by one of the larval stages of various species of flukes (fig. 7-18). The infestation may occur in freshwater, brackish, or salt water.

The flukes are members of the phylum Platyhelminthes, which includes the class Turbellaria, the planarians; the class Cestoda, the tapeworms; and the class Trematoda, the flukes. Under normal circumstances, the definitive host of many fluke species are parasites of a wide variety of vertebrates, including human beings in some instances. In the case of marine schistosomal dermatitis, the definitive host is a marine bird or some other marine vertebrate.

The eggs of the fluke are dropped into the water and hatch into an early larval stage. This eventually invades a suitable marine snail, which serves as an intermediate host.

Medical Aspects: The larvae of the fluke, known as *cercariae*, are released from the snail, whereupon they seek out a suitable host for their further development. It is at this point that they become involved with

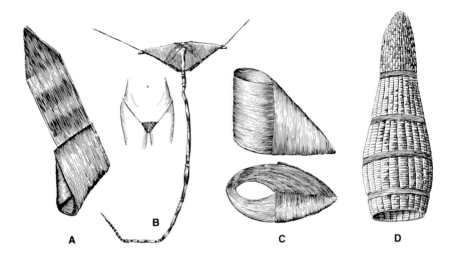

Fig. 7-17. Protective devices worn by natives to protect themselves from the parasitic candirú, and from schistosomal infections. *A*. Penis stulp worn by men of the Baoró tribe, Xingu River, Amazonia, Brazil. *B*. Wuri, or pudendal covering worn by Bakairi women, upper Xingu River. *C*. Penis stulp worn by men of the Kanapó and Tapairape tribes along the Araguana River, Amazonia. *D*. Protective device worn by the Zulus of Rhodesia to prevent penetration of the penis by the trematode parasite *Schistosoma*. Drawing by R. Kreuzinger, after Gudger.

human beings. Upon penetration of human skin the cercariae are capable of producing a severe skin reaction. At the site of entry an intense local foreign body reaction is produced, which results in the death of the larval fluke. The death of the larvae causes a reddened papular eruption with intense itching. Repeated infestations can cause severe hypersensitivity reactions.

The first symptoms of cercarial infestation usually occur as a prickling sensation either in the water, or soon after leaving it, possibly due to the mechanical irritation of the penetration of the skin. The sensation soon disappears, but a small red spot remains where the cercaria penetrated the skin. If the person is hypersensitive to these worms, the red spot becomes papular, inflamed, and swollen, accompanied by intense itching. Due to scratching or rubbing, the lesions can become severely infected. In most cases after several days the spots begin to fade, and in about a week only brown spots remain.

Schistosomal dermatitis has been reported in New South Wales and Northern Territory, Australia; Tasmania; Hawaii; and Florida.

Treatment: Antihistamines are useful in controlling the inflammatory reaction and the itching. Antihistamine and steroid creams provide prompt

Fig. 7-18. Cercaria of *Schistosoma japonicum* Katsurada. Original magnification ×448. Most of the cercarial dermatitis involving humans coming in contact with contaminated salt water are caused by helminth cercarial larvae, in which the native hosts are birds, marine mammals, or some other marine organism. This photo is shown only as an example of the morphology of the cercaria. When marine cercaria enters the host the tail is dropped off, but the life cycle of the organism is not completed. *S. japonicum* is generally found in freshwater and is the causative agent of Oriental schistosomiasis. Photo courtesy of the Armed Forces Institute of Pathology.

symptomatic relief. Antibiotics may be required to control secondary bacterial infections. The use of topical DMSO (dimethylsulfoxide) may also be helpful.

Prevention: Persons bathing in waters infected with flukes are advised to use protective clothing—either a heavy nylon or rubber diving suit. Dimethylpthallate solution (25 percent in a cream base) rubbed on the skin before swimming in an infested area is reported to be helpful in minimizing the cercarial infestation. Brisk rubbing with a rough towel immediately upon leaving the water is also helpful.

SELECTED BIBLIOGRAPHY

Ahmed, F.E., ed. *Seafood Safety: Institute of Medicine.* Washington, D.C.: National Academy Press, 1991.

Anderson, D.M., A.W. White and D.G. Baden, eds. *Toxic Dinoflagellates.* New York: Elsevier, 1985.

Auerbach, P.S., ed. *Wilderness Medicine: Management of Wilderness and Environmental Emergencies.* 3d ed. New York: Mosby, 1995.

Cafiero, G., and M. Jahoda. *Sharks: Myth and Reality.* Charlottesville, Va.: Thomasson-Grant, 1994.

Curtsinger, B. "Close Encounters with the Gray Reef Shark." *National Geographic* 187(1) (January 1995): 45-66.

Dunson, W.A. *The Biology of Sea Snakes.* Baltimore, Md.: University Park Press, 1975.

Ellis, R., and J.E. McCosker. *Great White Shark.* New York: Stanford University Press, 1991.

Hall, S., and G. Strichartz. *Marine Toxins: Origin, Structure, and Molecular Pharmacology.* Washington, D.C.: ACS Symposium Series 418, 1990.

Halstead, B.W. *Dangerous Aquatic Animals of the World: A Color Atlas.* Princeton, N.J.: Darwin Press, 1992.

_____. *Poisonous and Venomous Marine Animals of the World.* 2d rev. ed. Princeton, N.J.: Darwin Press, 1988.

Halstead, B.W., P.S. Auerbach and D. Campbell. *A Colour Atlas of Dangerous Marine Animals.* Boca Raton, Fla.: CRC Press, 1990.

Hamner, W.M. "A Killer Down Under: Australia's Box Jellyfish." *National Geographic* 186(2) (August 1994): 116-30.

Hui, Y.H., J.R. Gorham, and K.D. Murrell, et al., eds. *Foodborne Disease Handbook: Diseases Caused by Hazardous Substances.* New York: Marcel Dekker, Inc., 1994.

Mandojana, R.M., ed. *Clinics in Dermatology: Aquatic Dermatology.* Philadelphia: J.B. Lippincott, 1987.

Miller, D.M., ed. *Ciguatera Seafood Toxins.* Boca Raton, Fla.: CRC Press, 1991.

Ragelis, E.P., ed. *Seafood Toxins.* Washington, D.C.: ACS Symposium Series 262, 1984.

ographySELECTED BIBLIOGRAPHY

Russell, F.E. *Poisonous Marine Animals.* Neptune, N.J.: T.F.H. Publications, Inc., 1965.

Stevens, J.D., ed. *Sharks.* New York: Facts on File Publications, 1987.

Tu, A.T., ed. *Food Poisoning: Handbook of Natural Toxins.* New York: Marcel Dekker, Inc., 1992.

_____. *Marine Toxins and Venoms: Handbook of Natural Toxins.* New York: Marcel Dekker, Inc., 1988.

_____. *Toxin-Related Diseases: Poisons Originating from Plants, Animals and Spoilage.* New Delhi: Oxford and IBH Publishing Co. PVT. LTD., 1993.

INDEX

ABOUT THE AUTHOR

Dr. Bruce W. Halstead was born in San Francisco, California. He received a B.A. in zoology from the University of California at Berkeley and an M.D. from the Loma Linda University School of Medicine, and then served as assistant director of the School of Tropical and Preventive Medicine at Loma Linda University.

Now retired from clinical practice, Dr. Halstead has been an advisor to over twenty-five scientific, industrial, and governmental organizations worldwide. He has devoted his career to the scientific exploration of the environment, its nutritional resources, both marine and terrestrial, and human ecology. As a result he has traveled extensively and lectured for Project Ocean Search with the Jacques Cousteau Society for eighteen years.

The founding director of World Life Research Institute in Colton, California, Dr. Halstead studies dangerous marine animals, holistic preventive health care, nutrition, functional foods, development of famine foods, radiation sickness, immunology, AIDS, cancer, global pollution, aquaculture, horticulture, and traditional herbal medicine. He is currently participating in the development of a Marine Biotechnology Center in Ensenada, Mexico.

Dr. Halstead is the author of many books and articles, most notable being the five-volume work, *Poisonous and Venomous Marine Animals of the World,* which he spent thirty years researching and writing. He is currently working on books concerning drugs from the sea, and Chinese plants used in the treatment of AIDS, cancer, and radiation sickness.

In his spare time, Dr. Halstead enjoys restoring Model T Fords (1909-1928), developing hydrogen combustion engines, recovering refractory ores, and furthering his interest in horticulture.